DV 101

A Hands-On Guide for Business,
Government & Educators

Jan Ozer

DV 101
A Hands-On Guide for Business, Government & Educators

Jan Ozer

Peachpit Press
1249 Eighth Street
Berkeley, CA 94710
510/524-2178
800/283-9444
510/524-2221 (fax)

Find us on the World Wide Web at: www.peachpit.com
To report errors, please send a note to errata@peachpit.com

Peachpit Press is a division of Pearson Education

Developmental Editor: Stephen Nathans
Production Editor: Alan Reade
Copyeditors: Kinley Levack, Jackie Bennion
Proofreader: Evan Pricco
Compositor: Anna McBrayer, Amy Hassos
Indexer: Jan Ozer
Cover design: Mimi Heft
Interior design: Anna McBrayer, Mimi Heft

ISBN 0-321-34897-4

9 8 7 6 5 4 3 2 1

Printed and bound in the United States of America

For Barbara, Whatley, and Eleanor Rose

Acknowledgments

Regarding camera work, audio, and lighting, I'd like to thank Ken Santucci and Frank Grimaldi for their tech reads and suggestions. I couldn't have written the chapters on closed captions without the gracious help of Cynthia M. King, Ph.D., executive director, academic technology of Gallaudet University, and Andrew Kirkpatrick, project manager, WGBH National Center for Accessible Media.

Tom Smith, the sponsor for the seminars I teach for the University of Wisconsin, contributed many ideas on how this book could better serve university professors, engineers, and other professionals. I appreciate the feedback and ideas from the many professors and other university and governmental personnel who have attended these seminars over the years.

I owe a debt of gratitude to those who helped create this book, especially Stephen Nathans, my editor and running coach; Kinley Levack, my eagle-eyed copy editor; and Anna McBrayer, who designed the book and cover and typeset the book. Special thanks to Walt Fuller from St. Barthélemy Press, for his sage advice and counsel, and to Tom Campbell, from King Printing, who helped make the entire process seem easy.

Special thanks to Adobe, Apple Computer, Beachtek, Dell Computer, Epson, Hewlett-Packard, Innoventive Software, Media Access Group, Microsoft, Pinnacle Systems, Serious Magic, Shure, Sonic Solutions, Sony, Sorenson Media, Ulead Systems, Verbatim, and the WGBH Educational Foundation, who all supplied hardware or software for this book.

Thanks to the local folks from the Legacy of Mountain Music Association (LOMMA) for providing a fertile playground for experimenting with microphones and shooting techniques, and to Dr. Don T. Sumie for allowing me to use his interview in this book.

Finally, many thanks to Regina Kwon for marketing assistance and to Pat Tracy for technical and other assistance.

Table of Contents

Introduction

First of all, thanks for buying this book. I'll let you know what's available in the book and what you'll find on the Doceo Web site after a bit of background.

I had several goals with this book. Over the past few years, video departments in corporations, government offices, and academic institutions have been downsized, while the cost of high-quality DV gear, computers, and DVD recorders have dropped significantly. The amount of video work done by corporations and institutions, hasn't declined, but the work has been out of the hands of video specialists. Much of the shooting, editing, and producing video is now done by teachers, executives, staffers, and others who have little or no training in shooting with a camcorder, editing video, or producing a DVD.

I wrote this book to provide *specific* and *directed* production assistance to this new class of video producers. Not general theory, but details such as where to put the camera in a two-person training video, how to connect microphones, and which font to use in your titles.

My main aim was to provide a book that would help a complete novice shoot, edit, and output high-quality video to meet or exceed all organizational objectives—however reasonable or unreasonable.

To accomplish this, the book needed to provide both general knowledge and—where appropriate—software-specific guidance for those who need it. Unfortunately, if you include lots of software-specific direction within a book, you guarantee there will be content some readers don't want (e.g., Mac users glazing over screenshots of Windows-based programs), and the book will be obsolete soon after it hits the streets.

For this reason, I supplemented the printed book with downloadable PDF workbooks. These contain instructions on how to use particular tools to accomplish the tasks described in the book, as well as other support materials—some available for free, and some for a modest charge. Using the same projects illustrated in the printed book, these highly visual workbooks walk you through the production process, step by step, with program-specific screens illustrating each task.

If you're an experienced user, you probably won't need the workbooks. On the other hand, if you're just getting to know your chosen editor or authoring program, you'll probably find the workbooks extremely helpful. Go to *www.doceo.com/dv101.html* for a list of available workbooks.

A related note, you may notice in Chapters 5 and 8 that I include several software screenshots where I didn't name the program. This is because the screens were used to illustrate general principles applicable to many programs in each category, rather than features specific to the program shown. In addition, since program interfaces change so quickly and frequently, I didn't want to confuse readers with screens that no longer looked like the programs identified. I apologize if you found this lack of product identification irritating.

About This Book

The book is split into three major sections—shooting, output, and distribution-presentation. The first three chapters cover shooting, audio, and lighting, to help ensure that your productions start with the highest possible audio/video quality.

Chapter 4 goes into the theory behind the workflow of converting your raw DV footage to streaming video and DVDs. Then, Chapters 5 through 8 go into more detail about these procedures, with a look at the specialized subject of shooting for compositing and low-bitrate streaming in Chapter 6.

Once you've produced your video files, the focus shifts to distribution. Chapter 9 details how to insert videos into PowerPoint and Apple Keynote, while Chapter 10 describes how to create streaming presentations with PowerPoint Producer. Chapter 11 wraps up with a look at how to produce and deploy closed captions in streaming files and DVDs.

The book does not include reviews of DV cameras, video editors, or DVD authoring programs, or "how to" articles on buying or configuring your capture and editing station. This information changes too quickly to have much staying power in a book and you'll be better served by specialized magazines covering these topics.

If you're interested in this information, I invite you to visit *www.emedialive.com* and *www.pcmag.com*. The first site, EMedia, provides more lengthly reviews and analysis while PC Magazine provides quick-hit reviews of the most critical hardware and software tools.

Chapter 1:
Mastering the Video Shoot

It's axiomatic, but true: all video projects start with *someone* filming *something*. If that someone doesn't capture all the necessary shots and frame them correctly, you usually can't "fix it in post," and project quality suffers. Fortunately, with just a little advanced planning, you can get it right the first time and pretty much every time. That's what this chapter is about.

I'll start by outlining some assumptions I'll be using throughout this book, and then describe some common shooting scenarios that will serve as the templates for this first chapter, and the following chapters on audio and lighting. Then I'll describe how to create your "shot list," (the list of shots to take during and after your shoot), how and where to set up your camera, and how to frame your subject in the camera.

I'll finish with some recommendations regarding setting the scene: specifically, the types of backgrounds and clothing to avoid, and how different distribution media, like streaming video, should impact how you set your scene and shoot your video.

Assumptions

I'll be using these basic assumptions throughout the book.

*   *You may be flying solo*—I'll assume that many of you are both camcorder operator and onscreen interviewer (when applicable), so in some scenarios you won't be able to accomplish certain tasks, like panning the camcorder around the scene or zooming in and out. Since some readers may also have someone to drive the camcorder, I'll describe how to work solo and with a helper.

*   *You probably only have one camcorder*—Most shoots simply look better when shot with several camcorders, but I'll assume that you may have only one. I'll cover where to set the camera up and what to shoot in these instances, and also where to position and point additional camcorders if you have them available.

- *You're editing digitally*—I'll assume that you're editing the video on a computer, rather than simply playing back the video as recorded to tape. All computer editing systems are nonlinear, which means that you can place the sequences that you shot in any order in the finished video. This means that you can take your shots in the order that's most convenient, rather than having to shoot them in the order they will ultimately be used.

- *You're producing for professional distribution*—Whether you work for a corporation, university, government institution, or other organization, you're producing this video for enterprise use. You may not be trained in video production, but you're expected to produce professional results.

Three Scenarios

We'll use the following three scenarios in this chapter to describe how to set up the scene, sequence your shots, and frame the subject in the camera. In subsequent chapters, we'll revisit these scenarios to discuss how to light and mike each scene.

Of course, not all of your video shoots will fall neatly into one of these categories; there are weddings, sporting events, parties, and literally hundreds of other events that we shoot with our camcorders. Keep in mind that most of the rules below, particularly those relating to framing, apply equally to virtually any video shoot.

1. Executive Briefing

In an executive briefing, a company executive, educational administrator, or government official is talking directly to the audience. Because the subject is speaking directly to the audience, she looks and speaks directly towards the camera (**Figure 1.1**). As we'll discuss in more detail below, the subject is framed in the center of the image, with the eye-line approximately one-third of the way down from the top of the frame.

Figure 1.1. In the executive briefing scenario, the subject is speaking directly to the audience, so looks directly at the camcorder.

Use this scenario only when the subject is speaking directly to the audience. For example, in a person-to-person interview, the subject is speaking to and looks at the interviewer, not the camera. In terms of the videography techniques involved, a person-to-person interview is a different scenario entirely (see next section).

For this and the other scenarios, I'm using images generated by Innoventive Software's FrameForge 3D Studio, a program that produces storyboards, or pictures of sequential shots to help filmmakers visualize, plan, and execute the shots in their movies. To produce this simulated camera shot, I created a virtual set we'll look at later to study subject and camera positioning. In the meantime, to learn more about FrameForge, go to *www.frameforgestudio.com*.

2. Interview

In interviews the subject responds to questions from the interviewer and looks at this person, not the camera, as shown in **Figure 1.2**. Looking at the interviewer is much easier for most people, who freeze up when a video camera is pointed at their face.

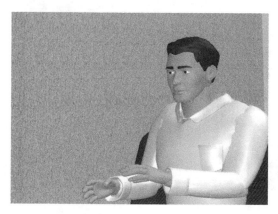

Figure 1.2. During the interview, the subject should look at the interviewer, not the camera.

3

Unlike group discussions, where the comments of all participants are more or less equally important, interviews are designed primarily to get the comments of the interviewee in the video. Consequently, they follow different rules. Use this scenario when creating a customer testimonial or interviewing an important visitor to your corporation or campus. Your role as interviewer is less important than that of the subject, so the interviewee gets most of the camera time. Note that the interview scenario is used frequently on the evening news, which makes it a great place to learn and refine your techniques.

In this scenario, I'm assuming that most readers are both cameraperson and interviewer. For this reason, the camera should stay focused on the subject during most of the interview. Even if you do have a separate cameraperson, it's tough to shift the camera smoothly from one person to another, and so it's best to keep it on the subject. Don't worry, we'll get you into the picture by shooting "noddies" after the interview is over; more on this below.

3. Discussion/Training

In a discussion or training scenario, two or more people are talking, and all of them are equally important to the shot. In a one-camera shoot where one of the participants is also a cameraperson (and thus can't be moving the camera around to focus on the different speakers), this means the camera must stay focused on the entire group all the time.

The discussion scenario, with one possible configuration shown in **Figure 1.3**, is the broadest; it can encompass conferences, group discussions, training sessions, role-playing, and other instances where all people must be on camera all the time. If you have only one camera, the rules are pretty much the same whether you have two participants or five. You basically have to keep everyone on camera all the time.

Figure 1.3. The discussion scenario, in which all participants must be on camera all the time.

Creating Your Shot List

Once you've identified your scenario, it's time to plan your shoot. Nowhere is Stephen Covey's second skill of highly effective people (begin with the end in mind) more important than in video production. In most instances, if you don't shoot the necessary footage the first time around, you can't go back to get it later.

For this reason, before you shoot, you should start with a very solid vision of what the final video will look like from start to finish. Then you should compile a list of shots, like the one shown in **Table 1.1**, that are necessary to fulfill the vision.

As we discussed above, the order in which you shoot your scenes is not important. All nonlinear editors can easily cut and paste videos as necessary to produce the finished video. What is critical is that you create the list, and shoot the shots.

Table 1.1. A shot list for our physician recruitment example.

Shot #	Duration	Purpose	Description
1-5	20-30 seconds each	Diverse clients	Patient shots (at least five patients of varying ages and ethnic backgrounds)
6-9	20-30 seconds each	Wide practice	Performing different diagnostic procedures (three to four) or using different devices
10-13	20-30 seconds each	Infrastructure	Working with a nurse, on the computer system, and with a dictation machine
14-16	20-30 seconds	Reasonable working hours	Turning out office lights, leaving building, and getting into car
17	2 minutes	Ambient noise	Shot of nothing (a Seinfeld shot) to capture ambient audio to use during editing
18	5-10 seconds	Establishing shot	A shot showing the clinic building
19	5-10 seconds	Establishing shot	A shot of the clinic sign
20	Multiple, 5-10 seconds each	Noddies	Shots of the interviewer reacting to the subject's answers
21	As necessary	Noddies	Shots of the interviewer asking questions

Telling Your Story—Visually

Two different elements contribute to the shot list. First are the shots necessary to visually tell the story. Consider the interview. Perhaps you're interviewing a customer to produce a customer testimonial. You could produce a video showing only the customer describing the benefits your product or service delivered, but this would be visually uninteresting.

A better approach is to complete the interview, and then get additional shots to visually illustrate the key points made by the customer. Using a technique called "insert editing" described in Chapter 5, you can then insert that video into the movie. While the viewer hears the subject describing your product's benefits, she sees the benefits onscreen. That's visual storytelling.

For example, suppose I was creating a recruitment video for a family practitioner to come live and work here in Galax, Virginia. The centerpiece of the production is an interview with a local family practitioner describing why he enjoys working and living in Galax.

Before I show up on site, I would ask the doctor why he enjoyed practicing in Galax. Let's assume the positive points he mentioned include an interesting base of clients, pursuing a diverse practice not limited by the specialization found in big cities, reasonable working hours, and an infrastructure that minimized paperwork and other hassles.

From this information, I would start creating a list of shots necessary to illustrate these benefits, as shown in Table 1. In TV jargon, completing the shots on this list would be called getting "coverage," or the footage necessary to tell the story. These shots may also be called "B-Roll" or "cutaways"—shots ancillary to the primary subject of the video, which in this case is the interview.

Visual Continuity—Outside/Inside

You should also plan to take shots that enhance the visual continuity of the video; this helps the viewer keep track of what's going on. For example, most interviews or other news items start with an establishing shot that shows a big-picture view of the shoot. You'll note that the shot list in Table 1 calls for two establishing shots.

Rather than starting my recruitment video with interview footage, I'll start with a shot of the clinic building, followed by a close up of the sign in front of the building. This lets viewers know that we're shooting in a doctor's office and that the person they'll soon see is a physician.

Figure 1.4. Telling the story visually.

Figure 1.4 shows the result. The shots of the clinic and sign last only three or four seconds each, but quickly let viewers know where they are and with whom they'll be talking. The video continues with some interview footage, interspersed with other clips to back up the doctor's statements. Not only does the additional video give credence to those statements, the pace of change helps keep the viewer interested in the video. The resulting video is much more compelling than sequential shots of the physician answering questions.

Establishing/Re-Establishing

The first time you shoot any footage in any environment, start with an establishing shot that illustrates the environment to the viewer. Then you can zoom into a medium shot, typically defined as any shot that shows mid-chest to the top of the head; this is about as close as you want to get with most executive briefing shots.

Every few minutes, zoom back to a wider shot, often called a re-establishing shot, to remind the viewer where the video is taking place. This sequence is shown in **Figure 1.5**.

Figure 1.5. Establishing shot on the left, medium shot in the middle, and re-establishing shot on the right.

This is easy if you're shooting an executive briefing, since you can work the camera and make the adjustments, but if you're both the cameraperson and a participant in a group discussion or interview situation, getting up and adjusting the camera can break the flow of the conversation.

Oftentimes, I'll bring a small television set to the interview, which I connect to the camera and use to monitor the shot—out of sight of the interviewee, of course. Then I use the camera's remote to zoom in and out, which generally works well. Otherwise, to reframe the shot, or zoom the video in or out, I'll stop the interview or discussion—claiming a "sound check" or other equipment check—adjust the camera, and restart.

A couple of caveats: First, slow zooms don't work well when you're producing video for (for example when you're outputting for the web streaming). These camera motions can cause visual artifacts (usually an exaggerated pixelated effect) in the video. So, when shooting for streaming, make the zoom adjustment as quickly as possible, perhaps even in a gap between questions; which you can then cut out during editing.

Second, long establishing shots don't work well for streaming either, since the eventual video viewing window is so small. When shooting for Web streaming, it pays to stay closely framed in on the subject, so that he or she almost completely fills the screen, and the talking head looks as large as possible.

Finally, beware of framing the camera too close when you're both cameraperson and interviewer. If your subject shifts slightly in her seat, she can move out of the picture or disrupt the framing. As I mentioned earlier, when I'm doing double duty as cameraperson and interviewer, I often bring a small television to display the output from the camera. I place it where I can see it, and where the interviewee can't, and use it to make sure the framing doesn't get away from me.

Two-Shot/One-Shot

In an interview setting, you should also try to start with a shot showing both you and the interviewee in the interview location, usually called a two-shot. Then you can switch to the shots of the subject that comprise the bulk of the video.

In **Figure 1.6**, the woman on the left is interviewing the subject on the right. The first shot in the sequence should be the two-shot shown on the left, which helps the viewer understand the physical setup. After displaying this shot, you can jump to the shot of the subject on the right.

Figure 1.6. The two-shot/one-shot interview sequence.

In a one-camera shoot with a separate cameraperson, it's pretty simple. As shown in **Figure 1.7**, (a top-down view of the interview set), you shoot the two-shot from Position A, then move to Position B for the bulk of the interview.

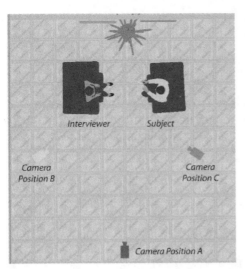

Figure 1.7. The three camera positions in an interview setting.

If you're running both the camera and the interview, set the camera on its tripod, frame the two chairs, and start shooting. Then, take your seat and start chatting with the interviewee about preliminary subjects to get the two-shot. Don't worry about audio at this point; plan on recording a voiceover back at your studio to use with the two shot ("Today I met with Bill Clinton, author of My Life. Here's what he had to say about the book"). See Chapter 2 for more on audio recording.

I usually get the two-shot early on, before starting with the real questions. Then, I shift the camera to Position B and get started.

Getting the Noddies

When I want to include myself on camera in the final interview footage, I conclude the interview, say goodbye to the guest, and switch to camera Position C. There, talking to the open chair, I ask key questions again, and nod, smile, or look sympathetic, as if in response to the subject's answers. These are called noddies, and later, during editing, I'll insert them seamlessly into the final video.

In some instances, such as interviews in the subject's office, you can't stick around to shoot the noddies, so you'll have to shoot them back in your office. This works well when you can duplicate the background of the original shoot; if not, frame the camera closely so that the background shown is minimal.

Noddies add a professional touch by making it appear that the shoot involved several cameras, one continuously trained on you, the other trained on the guest. Noddies also add an interesting element to the video—your response to the subject's answers—and break up the interview footage. This is essential if you don't have sufficient B-Roll.

If you plan to shoot the noddies back in your office, it's essential to shoot a minute or so of ambient sound at the interview location, also known as "room tone." Otherwise, when you insert your questions during editing, they'll sound noticeably different from your subject's answers.

For example, when I shot the doctor in his office, there was a buzz of patients in the waiting room, Muzak on the speakers, and frequent voices of other doctors and nurses coming and going. To capture this, I simply left my camera running for two minutes while I was packing up. Then, when I recorded my noddies and questions back in my office, I imported this audio as background to my questions and nods, and they sounded as if they had been shot on location.

Audio Continuity

While on the subject of audio, let's address the issue of audio continuity. Typically, this isn't an issue when it comes to interviews or testimonials, since the audio will exclusively be either your voice or that of your subject. You'll insert cutaways without audio, using your voices for audio, so audio continuity is never broken.

However, maintaining a consistent audio stream can be a significant problem in event videography. For example, say you're doing a wedding and shooting folks dancing at the reception. Over the course of 15 or 20 minutes, you take multiple shots of the bride, groom, and key guests, which you intend to edit down to three or four minutes.

Each shot is two to ten seconds long, which is fine visually. However, if you retain the audio captured with each shot, when you edit them together, you'll have a cacophony of different songs, or the same song at different times.

To avoid this, make a point of shooting one song in its entirety, from start to finish. This song will serve as the background audio for all dance clips inserted into the sequence. While you may need to capture separate songs for both slow and fast dancing, typically you can fit most dance shots into one category or the other.

Setting the Scene—Executive Briefing

With this as prologue, let's set the scenes, starting with the executive briefing scenario shown in **Figure 1.8**. There are six issues to consider in setting the scene, with the first four identical in all three scenarios.

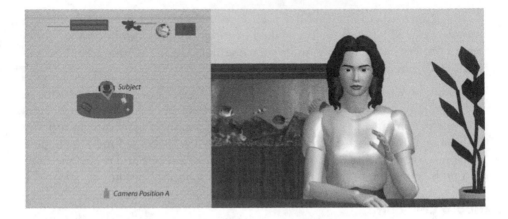

Figure 1.8. Setting the scene for the executive briefing and the Rule of Thirds as applied to a sub-

Whenever possible, scout the location beforehand (or at least ask about it) to identify any potential issues. Also, arrive as early as possible on the day of the shoot to give yourself time to assess and address environmental issues.

Locating the Subject

• When setting up the furniture, place the tables and chairs as far from the background as possible; this will help focus the viewers' attention on the subject. Also, when zooming in for medium shots and close-ups, the camera will focus on the subject, not the background. This approach can slightly blur the background, for a pleasing effect. As you can see in Figure 1.8, the subject is sitting several feet from the background wall.

Dressing the Subject

• The subject(s) should wear simple clothing with little detail. Avoid fine pin-stripes, herringbone patterns, and tweeds. These types of garments can create moiré patterns that shimmy in the camera. The result is not only distracting but can produce horrendous artifacts when compressed to high levels for streaming.

• Avoid high-contrast clothing like a white shirt with a black suit and red tie, since this stresses the camera's ability to accurately capture such a wide range of colors. It's best to stick with natural tones like browns and blues, and to tell your subjects this beforehand so they can dress accordingly.

• On location, ask the subject(s) to remove all shiny jewelry, which can flare up under the lighting.

Managing the Background

- Keep the background simple and clutter-free. Avoid finely detailed wallpaper, rows of books, and Venetian blinds, which can also produce a moiré pattern.

- Don't shoot against a blank wall, which can produce a range of artifacts, or defects. Keep the background spare and simple, as shown in Figures 1.1, 1.3, and 1.6.

- Avoid shooting against unshaded windows, since light streaming in can back-light your subjects, darkening the faces considerably.

- Turn off analog computer monitors, which typically scroll vertically in the video. Note that the newer LCD digital monitors don't do this, so if you need a computer monitor visible, switch to an LCD panel.

- If you're shooting to deliver over the Internet, consider using a dark flat background (black, dark blue) with nonreflective, light-absorbing material like velour or muslin. More on this in Chapter 6.

Camera Height

- In general, the camera should be placed at approximately the same height as the subject's face.

- Pointing the camera down at your subject makes him look subservient (but can hide a double chin).

- Pointing the camera upward makes the subject appear dominant or heavenly; notice how many political advertisements are shot in this manner!

Camera Placement

- The camera should be placed at least 10 feet from the subject—getting too close can distort the image.

- The only caveat is sound; specifically, if you're relying on the camcorder's microphone as your primary audio source, you'll need to get as close as possible to capture adequate sound.

- In the executive-briefing scenario, the subject will occupy the center of the frame, so the camera should be directly in front of and facing her.

Framing

As I've mentioned already; framing refers to where the subject is located within the camera frame. In the executive briefing, the subject is placed in the center of the frame, as shown on the right in Figure 1.8, with the eyes roughly one third of the way down the frame. This is one application of the Rule of Thirds.

Framing also describes how closely the camera zooms into the subject. Figure 1.8 is generally considered a medium long shot, since it shows the subject from the waist up. A medium shot is generally from the chest and up, and the closest you would want to frame an executive briefing.

That's because close-ups are used to show emotion or the subject's reaction to what another person is saying. As no one else is talking in the executive briefing, and in the absence of a Tammy Faye Bakker-style confession, shots that display emotion shouldn't be an issue.

Interview

In the interview setting, most footage—including that of the subject and the interviewer's noddies—will be shot with the two parties facing each other, not the camera. For these shots, you'll position the camera as shown on the left in **Figure 1.9**.

Figure 1.9. Setting the interview scene and using the Rule of Thirds to create "look room."

To recap, Camera Position A is for the initial two-shot where you'll center the subject and interviewer in the camera. Then you'll move to Position B for the bulk of the interview, with the camera set up and pointing at the subject at about 30 degrees from the line between the subject and interviewer.

When the subject is not directly facing the camera, the Rule of Thirds dictates how the shot is framed so that the subject's eyes are located at one of the four "saddle points," or those points in the frame where the lines intersect. In Figure 1.9, I've framed the shot to place the subject's eyes in the upper right saddle point, because that leaves "look room" toward the left, in the direction the subject is facing. This enhances the desired impression that the subject is looking at the interviewer.

If you're using a separate cameraperson, shoot the two-shot from Camera Position A, then move to Position B. Shoot an establishing shot showing the subject and the chair, then zoom into medium-shot territory, shooting from the chest up. Zoom out a little if the subject moves his or her arms like John Madden, so the picture won't constantly cut off the motion.

At intense or emotional points in the interview, don't be afraid to zoom into a close-up of the face, but linger for only a few seconds. Close-ups are interesting garnish, but shouldn't be a staple of your production.

Once the interview is over, it's time to move the camera to Position C and shoot the noddies. When framing the picture, I place the interviewer in the upper-left saddle point, leaving look room on the right, or in whichever direction she is facing (**Figure 1.10**). During editing, when you cut from a shot of the subject to a shot of the interviewer, it looks like they're facing each other, which is the desired effect.

Figure 1.10 Shooting the noddies, leaving look room in the other direction.

Discussion

When shooting a multisubject discussion with one camera, use Camera Position A, as shown in **Figure 1.11**, a straight-on shot of the two (or more) participants. Frame the subjects in the center of the camera with their eyes positioned in the upper-third of the frame.

If you have additional cameras, position them across from the target (Camera B focused on the interviewee on the right, Camera C focused on the interviewer on the left), and a few degrees off center.

Figure 1.11. The discussion shot head-on from Camera Position A.

When framing these shots, use the Rule of Thirds to position each subject's eyes at the back saddle point, leaving look room towards the front. This is shown in **Figure 1.12**. As in the interview settings, close-up shots of the subject's face are appropriate in small doses, but stick with medium shots (chest and up) for the bulk of the discussion.

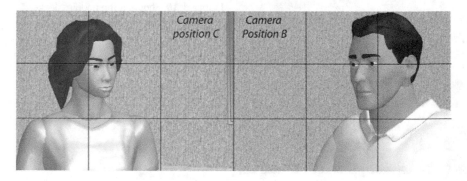

Figure 1.12. When working with multiple cameras, use the Rule of Thirds to place each subject's eyes in the back saddle point.

Multiple-Camera Shoots

There's no doubt about it—working with multiple cameras in a discussion scenario extends your creative options and makes both shooting and editing a lot more fun. If you have two cameras and someone to drive them, it's pretty simple to achieve, even with just one operator. Follow these pointers for the best results:

- Both cameras should be on tripods and should stay in the same physical position at all times. Trying to move a camera can throw off the discussion.

- Keep one camera (the primary camera) in Position A at all times. If you have one "good" camera and one "not so good" camera, make the good camera the primary one. If you have one "good" tripod and one "bad" tripod, use the bad one here, since the camera won't be moving.

- Keep the other (secondary) camera in either Position B or C and use it exclusively for medium shots and close-ups of the participants. Use your best tripod on this camera as you'll be panning and zooming throughout the shoot.

- If possible, the primary camera should capture all the audio, while the audio from the secondary camera should be used for backup or discarded.

- Start both cameras and keep them running the entire time. That will simplify synchronizing the video from the second camera to the audio from the first camera.

- While shooting, operate the secondary camera most of the time, but periodically check back on the primary camera to ensure it's running and the framing hasn't been jostled out of place.

- Tape all cords around both cameras to the floor, and make sure the path between the two cameras is free from obstacles. Be especially careful when moving around the primary camera to avoid knocking it out of position.

In the Workbook

Here's what's included in the workbook materials for Chapter 1.

I.   Shot List—a generic shot list to use when planning your shoot.

II. Storyboards—diagrams of shots and camera placement to use in planning your shoots. There's one for each of our three scenarios:

   A. Executive briefing

   B. Formal interview

   C. Two- or more-person discussion

Chapter 2:
Capturing High-Quality Audio

It generally takes a couple of video shoots before you realize that the weakest link on your camcorder is the microphone. Don't worry; it's not you, or your camcorder for that matter. It's just a simple fact of life that all onboard microphones are lousy.

This leaves you with two alternatives for capturing higher-quality audio: Get really close to your subject, or use an external microphone. Assuming that close proximity is not always an option, we'll look at a variety of microphone options that should provide a significant improvement over what you get with your camcorder.

We'll start with a brief inventory of your camcorder, which will tell us the type of microphones you can connect to and the equipment you'll need to do so. Then we'll survey the most popular types of microphones and their uses, and conclude with a brief look at several common shooting scenarios and recommend a specific microphone setup for each.

The good news is there are myriad options for working around your camcorder's microphone. For the most part, we'll look at the least expensive options, which can be operated by the cameraperson, and traveled with, or attached to, the camera. If you're permanently mike-ing up a room, you should consider a different range of options; but if you're assembling a kit you can afford and are able to take on the road at a moment's notice, you're in the right place.

BeachTek, Shure, and Sony provided most of the equipment we tested in this chapter, which is why their names keep popping up in the recommended equipment list. While they're certainly not the only suppliers out there, we're more comfortable recommending equipment that we've used multiple times and in the tests described below and several other shoots.

Identifying Your Connection Options

There are two ways to connect external microphones to camcorders, though not all camcorders offer either or both options. First is the microphone port, which comes in the two general categories shown in **Figure 2.1**.

Figure 2.1.
Camera microphone connectors.

XLR Connector   1/8" Stereo Connector

On the left is an XLR connector, which is typically available only on high-end prosumer and professional camcorders. On the right is the more typical 3.5mm stereo connector (also called 1/8" connector), which is found on most consumer camcorders.

If you study the image on the right in Figure 2.1, you'll note that the connector on this particular camcorder, a Sony DCR-VX2000, offers both MIC and LINE input, while the vast majority of consumer cameras offer only microphone input. Here's the difference.

Microphone-level input (MIC) is the sound produced by the inexpensive, primarily unpowered microphones such as those you may have used to record audio to your computer. They're inexpensive, and push out a very weak signal, only a few ten-thousandths of a volt. In contrast, line-level (LINE) power is produced by a powered sound system such as your stereo or a professional sound system. The signal is much, much stronger.

If your camcorder has MIC-level input (which it probably does if it doesn't say LINE), it should work well with many of the microphones we'll discuss here. However, if you ever try to connect your camera to a professional sound system, such as those that used at a speech or conference, you'll need to reduce the line-level output to microphone-level (more on this in the scenarios below). If you don't, the signal will be too strong for your camera and will produce distortion and possibly damage your camera.

The other detail you'll notice on the right in Figure 2.1 is the notation PLUG IN POWER beneath the MIC/LINE switch. Some microphones use "condenser" pick-ups to acquire and convert sound to electrical signals. Unlike dynamic microphones, which are driven by magnets and sound waves, condenser microphones need electrical power to produce a signal.

Connect a condenser-type microphone to a camcorder without plug-in power and you won't get a signal; that's all there is to it. There are alternatives for powering these types of microphones, but before choosing one, figure out whether your camcorder has plug-in power or not. Generally, if it doesn't say so on the microphone port, it doesn't have it, but check your camera's documentation to be sure.

Note that plug-in power supplies only 3.5 volts of power, sufficient for small consumer microphones using a mini-jack connector. However, most professional microphones require what is known as "phantom power," which supplies 48 volts. If you plan to connect a professional microphone to your camcorder, you'll need a device to supply this added power such as BeachTek's DXA-8, discussed below.

On the right in **Figure 2.2**, you can see the metal connectors beneath the covering I've pulled back, which indicates that the accessory shoe is intelligent and can power and communicate with a microphone and flash attachment.

Figure 2.2.
Dumb vs. intelligent accessory shoes.

Typically, if the accessory shoe is intelligent, the camera vendor will offer at least one optional microphone, but check with the seller to be sure. When available, these microphones are easy to install and use, relatively inexpensive, and can noticeably boost the sound quality over that of the embedded microphone. Let's take a look at the types of microphones you should consider.

Choosing Your Microphone

Figure 2.3 shows a good cross section of the types of microphones you will use on your shoots. Let's briefly identify them, and then cover the three characteristics of microphones you need to learn more about before buying.

Shure Lavaliere (SM 11)   Sony Wireless Lavaliere (WCS-999)   Sony ECM-HS1   Sony ECM-Z37C

Shure Boundary (EZB/O)   Shure Handheld (SM63)

Figure 2.3. An assortment of different microphone options.

On the bottom of Figure 2.3 is a handheld microphone, the Shure SM63 ($198 list), and similar to the mikes frequently seen on game shows and news broadcasts. As the name suggests, it's meant to be held in your hand during operation.

When you can use a handheld microphone, it's almost always the best alternative, with a great blend of quality and ease of use. It works well in many one- or two-person shoots, or when one interviewer is talking to multiple interviewees. You can also attach them to stands for hands-free operation in speeches, concerts, and conferences.

Just above the handheld microphone is a boundary microphone, the Shure EZB/O ($188 list). These microphones, also known as surface-mount mikes, are designed to be attached to desks or stage floors to pick up sound from multiple speakers and are typically used in conference rooms and theatrical plays.

Moving clockwise are two lavaliere microphones. These are designed to be attached to a single individual, and used hands-free. The Shure SM 11 Lavaliere ($175 list) is a "wired" lavaliere connected to the camera via a cable, while the Sony Wireless Lavaliere is part of the Sony WCS-999 wireless microphone system ($149.99 list) that sends the sound over a wireless signal to a receiver mounted on the camera.

Lavalieres are an excellent choice when you have one or two individuals speaking; they offer a great blend of quality and unobtrusive, hands-free operation. However, they're tough to transfer smoothly from person to person during the shoot. And, because they're smaller, lavalieres are less robust than handheld microphones, so they typically don't last as long.

To the right of the lavaliere are two microphones for mounting on a camera's accessory shoe. On top is the Sony ECM-HS1 ($69.99 list), which you connectvia an intelligent accessory shoe, and beneath it is the Sony ECM-Z37C ($149.99 list), which you connect via the attached cable using a 3.5mm adapter.

While the HS1 can only work on Sony camcorders with *intelligent* accessory shoes, the Z37C can work with any camcorder with an accessory shoe and a microphone port. If the camera's microphone port doesn't supply plug-in power, a small battery can power the Z37C.

These two Sony microphones share several characteristics. First, they are both "shotgun" microphones designed primarily to pick up sound from directly in front of the camera and eliminate sound from the sides and behind the microphone. Interestingly, in addition to "shotgun" mode, you can also switch the HS1 into "zoom" mode, where the pattern of sound picked up by the microphone mimics the current view of the camera's zoom lens. When the zoom lens is pulled completely back into a wide-angle view—say, to show an entire stage—the sound pickup pattern is also very wide. When the lens is zoomed in telephoto mode to focus on a single performer, the microphone pattern is similarly focused, eliminating all sound except that directly in front of the camera.

As we'll see, shotgun microphones produce better sound than most camcorder microphones, but are inferior to handheld and lavaliere microphones. While generally more flexible and easier to use than handhelds or lavalieres, shotguns aren't your best choice if quality is your primary goal.

Questions Before Buying

This leads us to the three questions you need to ask before buying a microphone. Note that you have to ask the same questions whether the microphone is wired or wireless, since the same issues arise with each.

1. What is the Pickup Pattern?

The pickup pattern, or directionality, of the microphone defines which sounds the microphone picks up and which ones it ignores. At one extreme are the "omnidirectional" microphones built into your camcorder that pick up sound equally from all sides of the camcorder. At the other extreme are "unidirectional" microphones that pick up sound from a single direction, and shut out all other noises.

For some microphones, like the shotguns we've been discussing, the pickup pattern is obvious. Shotgun microphones are designed to ignore ambient sound, and are extremely one-directional. In specification sheets for shotgun microphones, you'll frequently see terms like cardioid, super-cardioid, or even hyper-cardioid pickup patterns, which designate increasingly greater exclusions of ambient sound to focus more completely on the sound directly in front of the microphone.

Most other microphones come in either omnidirectional or cardioid patterns, and you need to be careful to get the right microphone for the intended use. For example, if you're buying a boundary microphone for use on a lectern where you want just the speaker's voice picked up, choose a cardioid pattern. However, if you're buying a boundary microphone for a conference room where all participants must be heard, an omnidirectional microphone is a better option.

It's also critical to know the pickup pattern when using the microphone. For example, if you're using a hyper-cardioid shotgun microphone to pick up a group discussion, you probably won't capture the panelists at the periphery of the group. Similarly, a handheld microphone with a cardioid pattern will eliminate sounds not emanating from directly in front of the top of the microphone.

2. Should I go Powered or Unpowered?

The next essential fact is whether the microphone requires power or not. As we discussed previously, if the microphone requires power, and your camcorder's microphone doesn't offer plug-in power, you'll have to figure out another way to power the microphone.

Most microphones that need power simply list "Phantom Power Requirements" or something similar on the specification sheet. All condenser-type microphones need power, either from the camcorder or battery. In contrast, dynamic microphones do not need power and can run even if your camcorder doesn't offer plug-in power—assuming your camera gives you some way to connect it, of course. Which leads to our next essential consideration: connector type.

3. What's the Connector Type?

Virtually all professional microphones connect via an XLRM connector, which is shorthand for XLR male. This means that the three XLR pins are sticking out of the connector and that your cable will need a corresponding female connector to attach to the microphone. Birds and bees at eleven.

XLR is a favored technology because it is "balanced," which means cables can run long distances without picking up noise from electrical wires and other sources. In contrast, unbalanced cables, such as those typically terminated with 3.5mm jacks, pick up noise easily, especially as cable lengths grow.

For this reason, you'll rarely see microphones that connect via 3.5mm plug—apart from the shotgun microphones that mount directly on your camcordes. The other primary exceptions are wireless microphones such as the Sony WCS-999 shown in Figure 2.3, which uses a 3.5mm jack to connect to your camcorder. However, since the receiver mounts on your camcorder, the distance traveled over the unbalanced wiring is relatively short.

Fitting a Square Peg into a Round Hole

If you want to use a high-end microphone with your camcorder, you'll have to find a way to convert from the XLR cable to the 3.5mm connector on your camera. Let's explore two alternative ways to achieve this.

The first is a "line-matching transformer" from Radio Shack—specifically the A3F XLR Jack-to-1/4" Plug Adapter/Transformer (part number 274-016c). Since this product outputs to a 1/4" plug, I added a 1/4"-to-3.5mm converter (part number 274-875A) to connect to my camcorder. The total cost was less than $20, not including the XLR cable. This rig is shown in **Figure 2.4**.

Figure 2.4.
The Radio Shack line-matching transformer. This right-angle setup looks almost painful.

In my lab, this setup generally works well, though it doesn't supply the phantom power required for many microphones. Ergonomically, however, it's clearly not a field solution, since one inadvertent bump would probably rip my camera into multiple pieces.

If I took the line-matching transformer route in the future, I would choose the Shure A96F transformer, which inputs XLR and outputs 3.5mm, with a flexible cable to avoid the awkward right-angle attachment shown in Figure 2.4. The mail order price for the A96F is around $40.

An even better alternative is the BeachTek DXA-8 "Ultimate Adapter" which lists at $399 but can be found for a few dollars less via mail order. **Figure 2.5** shows the two faces of the product, back and front. It screws into the tripod mount beneath your ocrew-camcorder, with a similar mount on the bottom so you can continue to use a tripod.

Figure 2.5.
Plug your cables into the front (top) of BeachTek's excellent DXA-8, with controls on the back (shown on bottom here).

On top, as you can see, the unit has three connectors, two for XLR cables and one for an unbalanced 3.5mm connector. The output is a 3.5mm connector with microphone power, so you can plug it into any camcorder with a microphone jack.

With the twin XLR connectors, you can use the DXA-8 to mix together two microphone signals, controlling respective volume with the two volume dials shown on the bottom of Figure 2.5. If you have two microphones, you can capture stereo audio. Even if you capture a monaural signal, as we did in our tests, the DXA-8 outputs the signal to both the left and right audio tracks. This doesn't create true stereo, but it does make sure that you have sound coming out of both speakers.

The 48V switch to the right of both volume controls indicates that the DXA-8, which is powered by a 9-volt battery, can supply phantom power to condenser microphones. In addition, the LMT buttons engage a "limiter" function that prevents distortion from hot inputs—this is a critical feature when accepting line-level input from a sound system. The unit also has preamplifiers to boost the low signal from microphones, which can also eliminate hiss.

After trying all these different approaches to converting XLR input, I have to say I like the BeachTek's under-the-camera approach the best. If you don't need all the functionality of the DXA-8, consider the DXA-2, which sells for around $125 and provides one XLR port and one unbalanced 3.5mm input, with volume control but no phantom power or limiters. I would definitely recommend this over the Radio Shack or even Shure A96F approach.

Performance Comparisons

Now you're well-versed on microphones and how to connect them to your camcorder, the obvious next question is how they perform in terms of quality. To test performance, we used a high-quality, digitized recording of a woman speaking, and played back over computer speakers at a standardized volume. To create ambient sound, we left all office equipment running, which created a distinct hum of background noise.

We set up the Sony VX2000 approximately 10 feet from the speakers, and then recorded the audio using the various microphones shown in Figure 2.3. During each recording, we used the VX2000's manual-gain controls to boost the audio to an acceptable level. While you'll notice some minor volume differences in the waveforms you're about to review, the most significant differences are found in the detail captured by the microphone and the amount of noise in the signal.

Let's start by looking at the difference between the best and the worst, shown in **Figure 2.6**, which contains waveforms produced by the camcorder microphone and the Shure Lavaliere microphone. You'll notice that the waveform on the bottom shows higher peaks and valleys, indicating higher volume. You'll also see that when there was no speech, on the right side of the waveform, the line of noise produced by the camcorder was thicker, indicating that it picked up more ambient noise from the room than the lavaliere, which translated to a more noticeable hum during playback.

Most striking, however, is the degree of detail missed by the camcorder. As shown in the picture, the speaker says the word "tutorial," and there are noticeable peaks at the Ts and I with the Shure Lavaliere. There are no such peaks in the camcorder's waveform, indicating that the onboard microphone's recording of the speech was muffled and hard to understand. If you listened to the results, you would find the Shure audio clear, crisp, and natural, while the camcorder audio would sound tinny—almost like it was shot in a barrel.

Overall, the results produced by the Sony wireless Lavaliere system, and the three Shure wired microphones were very similar and all of them clearly superior to the results produced by the two shotgun microphones. This is illustrated in **Figure 2.7**.

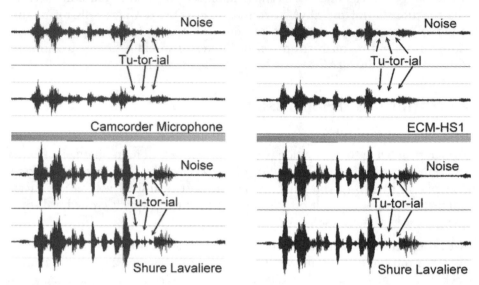

Figure 2.6. Comparing the quality of audio captured by the VX2000's microphone with the Shure Lavaliere.

Figure 2.7. Comparing the Sony ECM-HS1 shotgun microphone with the Shure Lavaliere.

Again, the Shure solution produced a higher volume, a crisper signal, and slightly less noise. Overall, while the ECM-HS1 and ECM-Z37C produced better audio than the camcorder microphone, the difference was much less striking than that produced by the microphones used closer to the source.

Don't take this as a sweeping indictment of all shotgun microphones. Both the Sony models are relatively inexpensive and rather small, and Shure, Sony, and other vendors offer larger, more sensitive models that would likely produce better results. In the price range we surveyed in this review, however, you'll produce the best results if you use or attach a mike at the source.

Now let's turn our attention to the difference in quality produced by connecting through the Radio Shack Line-Matching Transformer and the quality output by the BeachTek DXA-8. This is shown in **Figure 2.8**.

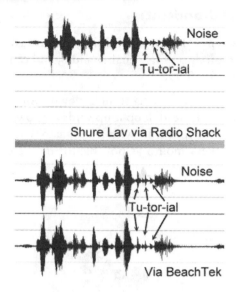

Figure 2.8.
Comparing the Lavaliere microphones output captured via Radio Shack and BeachTek products.

As you can see, the Radio Shack approach doesn't duplicate the monaural signal to both tracks, which is why there is only one waveform. To work around this, there are hardware adapters you can buy to duplicate the audio, otherwise you'll have to duplicate the channels in your audio editor to make sure you have sound coming from both speakers. The detail on the mono signal is quite good and slightly less noisy than the bottom signal, which was produced using the BeachTek unit.

The Radio Shack waveform creates less noise because its signal is lower than the BeachTek's, which sounds much more vibrant. The BeachTek signal is also much more nuanced than the Radio Shack signal, which sounds a bit flat. Overall, most listeners would clearly find the BeachTek audio the more pleasing of the two.

Real-World Sound Choices

With this as background, let's look at audio strategies for the shooting scenarios introduced in Chapter 1, as well as one or two others, and discuss the different microphone alternatives. I'll assume that your camera has a single 3.5" microphone connector that accepts microphone-level audio.

Scenario 1. Executive Briefing (CEO Broadcast)

Rig 1: Sony WCS-999 wireless lavaliere system ($149.99 list). This system is easy to operate and connect to your camcorder, produces high-quality audio, and can move around with the speaker. **Total Cost: $149.99.**

When using a lavaliere microphone, don't let the wire hang straight down, which can damage the microphone/cable connection. Instead, loop it upwards as shown on the right in **Figure 2.9**, and clip the cable to your shirt with the alligator clip. Mount the microphone as close to the speaker's mouth as possible for the best results.

Figure 2.9. The lavaliere microphone is perfect for this briefing.

Scenario 2: Formal Interview

Your needs here will vary with the number of cameras you use. If you're shooting with one camera, you can mount a lavaliere microphone on the subject during the interview, and then on the interviewer for the noddies and questions. A handheld microphone will deliver better quality than the camera's microphone, but is more intrusive than a lavaliere.

In a multiple-camera shoot, you'll need either two live microphones and a mixer unit, or a boundary microphone mounted on a table or desk between the two speakers.

Rig 1: Shure handheld microphone ($198 list), Shure AF96F ($40 list), 15-foot XLR cable ($14.99, Radio Shack). Speakers share the handheld microphone. Functional, good-quality audio, but not very elegant. **Total Cost (approximate): $260.**

Rig 2: Shure omnidirectional boundary microphone ($188 list), Shure AF96F ($40 list), 15-foot XLR cable ($14.99, Radio Shack). Hands-free operation; functional, good-quality audio. Room must be otherwise quiet, and the boundary microphones work best when placed on a raised desk or table. **Total Cost (approximate): $250.**

Rig 3: Two Shure SM 11 wired lavaliere microphones ($350 total, list), two 15-foot XLR cables ($30 total, Radio Shack), BeachTek DXA-8 ($399 list). Killer system with great quality and flexibility. **Total Cost (approximate): $800.**

Scenario 3: Group Discussion (interview, training)

Unlike the interview scenario, here we want both speakers on camera all the time, even if you only have one camera. The cheapest alternative is to have the speakers trade a handheld microphone, although for discussions longer than a few moments, this gets tiring pretty fast. **Figure 2.10** shows the dual-microphone approach.

Figure 2.10.
Dual handheld microphones work well in discussion settings, but look less elegant than dual lavalieres.

Rig 1: Shure handheld microphone ($198 list), Shure AF96F ($40 list), 15-foot XLR cable ($14.99, Radio Shack). Speakers share the handheld microphone. Functional, good-quality audio, but not very elegant. **Total Cost (approximate): $260.**

Rig 2: Shure omnidirectional boundary microphone ($188 list), Shure AF96F ($40 list), 15-foot XLR cable ($14.99, Radio Shack). Hands-free operation; functional, good-quality audio. Room must be otherwise quiet, and the boundary microphones work best when placed on a raised desk or table. **Total Cost (approximate): $250.**

Rig 3: Two Shure SM 11 wired lavaliere microphones ($350 total, list), two 15-foot XLR cables ($30 total), BeachTek DXA-8 ($399). Killer system with great quality and flexibility. **Total Cost (approximate): $800.**

Scenario 4: Wedding

Wedding requirements vary dramatically over the course of the celebrations—not to mention from venue to venue—and it's very difficult to propose one setup that works in all instances. At the very least, you'll need a microphone on the groom—either a wireless microphone like the WCS-999 or a MiniDisc or Digital Audio Tape recorder—and a shotgun microphone for the reception (or cabled or wireless handheld).

Since you may need to use the shotgun and lavaliere microphone simultaneously, you'll need a mixer like the DXA-8. The DXA-8 offers only one 3.5mm input, which you'll use for the wireless microphone, so you'll also need a shotgun microphone with XLR output—neither of the Sony units offers this.

Scenario 5: Connecting to a Sound System

If you're shooting a concert or conference, you'll get the best sound by connecting to the output of the on-site production sound system. In most instances, you'll have to solve at least two problems: physically connecting the soundboard to the camcorder, and dropping the line-level output to microphone-level input for your camera (assuming that it doesn't accept line-level input).

Depending on the soundboard, the outputs can be anything from RCA connectors such as those on your stereo, to 1/4" jacks or XLR connectors; make sure you're prepared for all three possibilities. We assumed XLR output for our suggested systems-setups.

Rig 1: The Shure A15LA Line Input Adapter ($42 retail) to drop the line-level output to microphone input and the Shure AF96F ($40) to convert from XLR to 3.5mm. This approach is less expensive, but there's no ability to adjust the sound coming from the sound system, which may still be pretty hot. **Total Cost (approximate): $80**.

Rig 2: BeachTek DXA-8 ($399). This unit can perform both conversions (XLR-to-3.5mm and line-to-microphone); it also offers limiters that help to ensure distortion-free audio, plus a ton of utility in other shooting environments. **Total Cost: $399**.

Cleaning Your Noisy Audio

When we created our test setup for this project, we deliberately left our computers, routers, printers, and monitors running, producing a consistent din of ambient noise. Our thinking was pretty obvious: how can you possibly test a shotgun microphone's ability to ignore ambient sound without lots of ambient sound?

Also, since few interviews or other types of videos are shot in sound booths, the noise also provided a lovely dose of reality.

Once we heard the background noise present in even our highest-quality recordings, our thoughts quickly turned to noise-reduction software. The software generally works best with regular, consistent background noise such as machine hum or tape rumble, as opposed to irregular noises such as cheering crowds or traffic noises. We surveyed our labs and checked recent press reviews, and rounded up three products.

First on our list was Sony's vaunted Noise Reduction filter for Sound Forge, which costs $280 direct, but requires Sound Forge ($399 direct) or another DirectX-compatible audio editor to run. Second was BIAS' newly released SoundSoap Pro for Windows ($599 retail) from BIAS, a DirectX plug-in we ran within Sound Forge. Third was the noise-reduction capability that comes with Adobe Audition, a complete audio editor that retails for $299, though it's much cheaper in several Adobe bundles.

Note that true noise-reduction filters work differently from inexpensive functions typically called noise gates. Briefly, the machine hum from my office equipment was most noticeable during the short periods between spoken words in the original recordings, though you can also hear it throughout the recording.

Noise gates work by setting thresholds for noise. When the audio exceeds the threshold, the noise gate filter assumes it's audio that is supposed to be heard and leaves it alone. When the volume goes under the threshold, it assumes the audio is noise, and simply eliminates it, reducing volume to zero.

When the speaker paused for breath in our test recording, a noise gate reduced the volume to zero, eliminating the hum during the otherwise silent period. However, noise gates do nothing to reduce the audible hum while the subject's speaking. This produces a noticeably artificial effect, since you can hear the hum when the subject's speaking, but not when she's quiet.

In contrast, all three noise-reduction technologies try to identify the background noise and eliminate it throughout the entire recording. You start by selecting an otherwise blank stretch in the audio file—one that's devoid of speech, music, or other audio that's supposed to be there, and contains only the background hum. Then you tell the noise-reduction filter to capture a noise "print" or profile of that hum, and eliminate it from the entire audio file. **Figures 2.11** to **2.13** show the noise profile captured by all three products.

We tested each noise-reduction technology on three audio files. We highlighted the same segment in the three original files to identify the noise print and then ran each filter using the default settings.

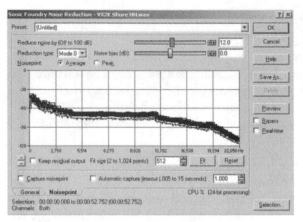

Figure 2.11.
Grabbing a noise print with Sony's Noise Reduction filter.

Figure 2.12.
SoundSoap Pro's highly effective eye candy.

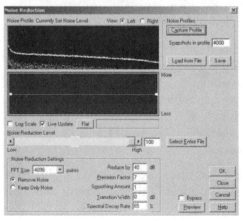

Figure 2.13.
Adobe Audition's competent Noise Reduction filter.

Two of the audio samples came from this project—first, the low-quality audio recorded with the embedded microphone on the Sony camcorder, and second, the excellent audio captured with the Shure handheld microphone. We also tested an audio file recorded from a cassette player.

On the high-quality recording, all three technologies virtually eliminated the machine noise, making it sound like it was recorded in a sound studio. The Shure microphone produced a great original signal, and all three filters made it sound positively pristine.

The results with the lower-quality recording were less impressive; basically, you can't turn a sow's ear into a silk purse, no matter how good your software is. Though all three programs removed most of the background noise, the detail that wasn't captured by the camcorder's microphone was not magically restored. While the recording sounded better, the improvement was incremental, not exponential. The lesson is clear: get a good microphone setup and don't expect to fix it in post.

The results from the cassette tape were simply fantastic, with all three products dramatically reducing tape hiss and rumble. If you're doing this type of conversion, noise-reduction technology should be in your budget.

Which product performed best? Very tough call and my instincts are to be politically correct on this one and say they were all equal, especially given the focused nature of our tests. In addition, since we used the default setting on all three products, it's impossible to say whether a bit of fiddling with any of the products would have produced significantly different results. However, if you held a gun to my head (or threatened to crush my beloved three-chip DCR-VX2000) I'd have to say that SoundSoap was shockingly good.

Happily, you don't have to put your money down based on this extorted recommendation; all three vendors offer free, downloadable trial versions that you can run on your own noise problems.

Jan's Rules

Here are the rules I've learned to live by when working with audio equipment in the field:

- The first time you use a new piece of equipment you're going to screw it up. So, you should perform at least one test shoot with anything new before you actually use it in an important shoot.

- You can't capture good audio without a good set of headphones. Ear buds are tempting because they're portable and unobtrusive, but they let the outside noise in, making it tough to differentiate between what the microphone is picking up and what you're actually hearing. For best results, get big, clunky "noise-canceling" headphones that block outside sound.

- If you're working a concert or conference, bring a small flashlight and some kind of tape to secure your audio wires or power cables.

- If you're picking up audio from the sound system, test out the system a few days before the event to make sure you have the proper connectors. Then arrive early the day of the event, to hook up and test again.

In the Workbook

The workbook for this chapter includes program-specific instructions on how to apply noise-filtering effects in each video editing program. Go to *www.doceo.com/dv101.html* for a list of currently supported video editors.

Chapter 3:
Guerilla Lighting

Good lighting is absolutely essential to shooting good video. However, if you're like me, 90 percent of the time you shoot your video without separate lights, using the sun (outdoors) or available lighting (indoors) as best you can.

Fortunately, a lack of lighting equipment doesn't prevent you from producing great video. However, though it might sound paradoxical (if not downright Zen), you must know how to work *with* lighting equipment to understand how to do *without* it; this allows you to optimize results by positioning your subjects or the available light for maximum effect.

I'll start by examining the two most common lighting combinations used on location and in the studio today. Then I'll discuss some lighting fundamentals to help arrive at a definition of what "good lighting" is. After all, you can't hit a target unless you know what it is.

Once we have a target, I'll discuss the tools available to help produce good lighting. Interestingly, one lovely characteristic of all video cameras is an absolutely egalitarian approach to lighting. Your camera doesn't care whether you spent thousands of dollars on your lighting equipment, or a few hundred, so long as the light is adequate and appropriately positioned. Accordingly, for those with $100 or so to spend, I'll describe how to buy highly effective lighting equipment at a fraction of the price of professional gear.

Finally, with all this as background, I'll describe how to apply what we've learned so far to our three scenarios and other common shooting situations you'll likely encounter in the field.

Three-Point Lighting—The Art of Lighting

Three-point lighting has its roots in lighting as art, rather than lighting as a necessary evil for a camera to do its work. The basic theory goes like this: Video is a two-dimensional medium served on a flat screen. Flat lighting, which lights each scene area equally, is visually uninteresting and serves only to emphasize video's two-dimensional nature.

To get around this, lighting should create "depth" within the video image and contrast between the foreground speaker and the background. The basic tool for accomplishing both goals is three-point lighting, as shown in **Figure 3.1**.

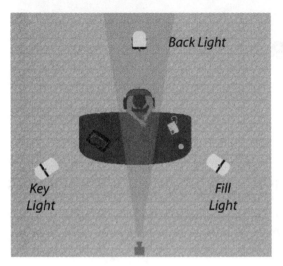

Figure 3.1.
Positioning your lights for three-point lighting.

The Key Light

As the name suggests, three-point lighting uses three lights. The key light is the primary light, and its job is to expose the shape of the subject; it does this by shining down on the subject from an angle, producing shadows, a technique also known as modeling.

As you can see in Figure 3.1, you position the key light at an angle of approximately 45 degrees from the camera, pointing directly on the subject. The light should be above the subject and shining down at an angle of about 45 degrees. A key light must be a "hard light" that produces shadows, but not so harsh that it creates excessive contrast between the lighted and the shadowed regions. I'll discuss hard and soft lights and lighting contrasts in depth in the Video Fundamentals section.

Positioning the key light is more art than science. When positioning this light, take note of the shadow cast by the nose, also referred to as the "nose caret," clearly visible in the key light image (left) in **Figure 3.2**. As a rule of thumb, the nose caret should never touch the lip (which means the light is too high) or protrude into the cheek area (which means the light is too far to the side).

You can position the key light slightly higher to produce shadows that hide a double or triple chin, but make sure the eyes remain clearly visible. This is a problem

Figure 3.2. Key light on left; key and fill light, center; key, fill, and back light on the right.

for me because my bushy eyebrows can block the light, making my eyes difficult to discern.

As you can see on the left in Figure 3.2, the key light did its job, producing a shadow that adds depth to my face. However, the contrast between the lighted area on the right side of my face and the shadows on the left is a little too strong. To moderate this, we'll add a fill light to "fill" the shadows.

The Fill Light

Where the effect of the key light is obvious, the fill light is more subtle, softly reducing the shadows produced by the key light rather than announcing the presence of another light. To accomplish this, the intensity of the fill light must be less than the key light, an effect you can produce by using a softer light or less powerful bulb, or by placing the light further from the subject.

As shown in Figure 3.1, the fill light should be placed at approximately the same angle as the key light, but on the other side of the camera. Placing the fill light at a different height from the key light will produce an asymmetry that enhances the desired modeling effect.

Compare the key light image in Figure 3.2 with the key and fill light image. You'll notice that the fill light did its job, softening the dark shadows produced by the key light, and revealing some of the detail on the left side of my face.

The Back Light

The back light is placed behind and shines down the subject. Rather than provide true lighting for the scene, the back light should produce a subtle halo on the top and back of the subject that provides contrast and visually separates the subject from the background, enhancing the three-dimensional appearance of the scene.

Ideally, you should place the back light directly opposite the camera and it should have the same intensity as the key light. If it's impossible to place the light directly behind the subject, place it on the side and shine the light down on the subject, or place a light on either side—both, of course, shining down onto the back of the subject. Be careful when positioning the light so that it does not also shine down on the camera lens—this can produce lens flares and even burn out pixels in the LCD viewfinder or panel.

If you look at the key, fill, and back light image in Figure 3.2, you'll notice that my hair and shoulders are lighted, providing contrast from the background. As discussed in the next section, though many television producers eschew three-point lighting for flat lighting, virtually all employ back lights to create this contrast.

So what are the takeaways of three-point lighting?

First, shadows are acceptable, if not desired. This is critical, because you can drive yourself crazy, especially out in the field, if you try to get rid of all facial shadows. By strategically placing the lighting and the subject, you can ensure that the shadows will enhance, rather than disrupt the image.

Second, uneven lighting is acceptable, if not desired. Again, don't go nuts trying to get even lighting on each subject's face. Rather, for reasons discussed more completely in Video Fundamentals, it's critical to limit the contrast between the brightest and darkest regions in the video.

Third, back lights are essential to separate the subject from the background, especially (in my experience) with indoor shots.

Flat Lighting—The Reality of Lighting

Open any book or article on lighting and you'll see a chapter or section on three-point lighting, usually identifying this technique as optimal, if not the be-all and end-all of professional lighting. However, there's one dark secret about three-point lighting that few sources reveal: most television programs don't use it.

Why? The reasons are plentiful. Three-point lighting usually requires high-powered incandescent lamps that consume capacious quantities of electricity, produce massive heat, and are tough on the subject's eyes. Three-point lighting is also very difficult to pull off when you have multiple subjects on screen simultaneously—especially if they're moving around.

Plus; with today's high-resolution, large-screen television sets, depth is more apparent, lessening the importance of three-point lighting. Finally, some producers obviously prefer to eliminate (or minimize) the nose carets and other shadows that three-point lighting produces.

So, while you may see three-point lighting in use in dramatic interviews on *60 Minutes*, you typically won't on broadcasts from ESPN, CNN, the *Tonight Show with Jay Leno*, the Golf Channel, and on most local news productions. All these programs use flat lighting, which minimizes shadows but retains the back lighting.

Producing flat lighting is very simple, as shown in **Figure 3.3**. Rather than using key and fill lights with different intensities, you use two key lights of identical intensity. And, rather than using hard lights that produce shadows, you use soft lights that produce less intense shadows.

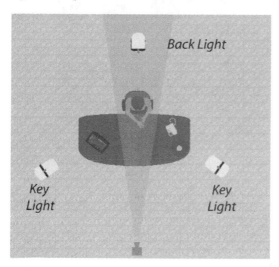

Figure 3.3.
Flat lighting using two equally powered key lights.

Flat lighting produces the image shown on the left in **Figure 3.4**, which has even lighting throughout the face and the characteristic shadow beneath the chin. On the right, I placed a bounce card (see Lighting Fundamentals section) on my lap to reflect the light back up to my face, noticeably reducing the chin shadow. Some producers use a fourth light, directly behind the camera, to accomplish this, but this approach places the light directly in the subject's eyes, which is tough going even for the pros.

So, what are the takeaways? Primarily, that flat lighting (casting no or minimal shadows) is certainly an acceptable way to go—an important consideration as it may be your only alternative in some indoor shoots. Some may find this contradictory to what we learned from examining three-point lighting, but I consider it supplementary.

While a documentary filmmaker may criticize your video if you use flat lighting, few, if any, nonprofessional viewers will even notice, any more than they notice the use of flat lighting on the evening news or *Jay Leno*. So when you're making do in the field, if flat lighting is all that's available—or the best option for providing good, consistent coverage—go with it. If you can implement three-point lighting effectively, go with that too.

Figure 3.4. Flat lighting: on the right used with a matte reflecting light under my chin to reduce shadow. Note to self: try some face powder to get rid of the shine.

Now let's take a quick look at some lighting fundamentals which will help round out our definition of good lighting.

Lighting Fundamentals

As you've seen, the mechanics of three-point lighting are fairly simple. However, unless you know what kind of lights to set up and why, your results will be suboptimal, if not downright disappointing. Here's what you need to know.

Your Camera Doesn't "See" As Well As Your Eyes

Just because your eyes can perceive details in a shot, doesn't mean that your camera can. Video is definitely *not* a What You See Is What You Get affair.

This reality causes problems primarily in scenes with "high-contrast" lighting—in other words the very significant differences between the brightest area in the shot and the darkest. Typically, you get excessive contrast when you're shooting a subject with extremely bright lights in the background, whether produced by the sun or a spotlight.

When you're looking at the scene with your eyes, you can see good detail at both extremes because your eyes have a contrast range of around 1,000:1. This compares to a contrast range of about 250:1 for the best video cameras, approximately 64:1 for cameras in the Sony VX2000 or Canon XL1 class, and as low as 30:1 in consumer camcorders.

Without getting too technical, this means that while your eyes will be able to perceive detail at both the darkest and lightest extremes, your video camera will not. This is why the left side of my face lost detail in the key light-only image in Figure 3.2. Simply stated, the contrast range between the darkest and lightest regions was too dramatic.

If too much lighting contrast exists in your scene, you have no good choices. If your exposure favors the darker area, the more lighted areas become washed-out blobs with no detail. If you adjust exposure to favor the lighter areas, darker regions turn completely black, and show no detail. Use an average exposure and you'll lose both extremes.

Interestingly, the "spotlight" or "backlight" control found on most camcorders doesn't really fix the problem. Rather, it simply tells the camera to ignore the bright background, and choose the best exposure for the face. While this restores some facial detail, you lose detail in the background, usually causing it to look slightly washed out. Spotlight and backlight controls are a great solution when you can't manage the lighting, but when you can, it's better to reduce the contrast range to acquire good detail and color throughout the scene.

Application:

- Alarm bells should start to ring if there are stark differences between the lightest and darkest regions in your video frame. This often occurs when shooting in direct sunlight around midday (which can produce very dark shadows), or when shooting subjects against bright windows or bright floodlights.

- You should also hear alarm bells when your subjects wear clothing with extreme ranges of contrast, such as a dark blue or black suit with a white shirt, or when people of color wear very light clothing or stand against a very light background. Once again, your camera can't preserve detail at both extremes, forcing you into damage-control mode.

- When it's practical, bring a television to help you judge scene lighting more effectively. It's very difficult to detect a loss of detail on your camcorder's 2.5" LCD, and most camcorder LCDs tend to produce brighter results than what actually appears on a television or computer. Relying on your camcorder's LCD panel, then, is a scary proposition.

All Lights Have a Different Color Temperature

Let's start with two fairly common situations to explain what this means:

Situation 1: You're shooting indoors, using sunlight streaming in from a window as your key light, and a lamp in the room as a fill light.

Situation 2: You're shooting indoors, lighting the scene primarily with fluorescent lights in the office ceiling, using an incandescent lamp to reduce facial shadows.

Now, as they say in law school, what result and why? Situation 1 is hopeless, and your subject's face will be either blue or orange. Same result in Situation 2 (unless you're very lucky), except that the face will be either overly green or orange. Now, the why.

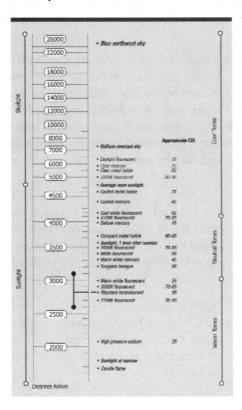

Figure 3.5. Color temperature and Color Rendering Index for common lighting types.

Simply stated, white is not "white" under all types of light. As shown in **Figure 3.5**, different lights produce slightly different coloring on the Kelvin scale, named after renowned Scottish physicist Lord Kelvin. The bottom of the scale, between 2,000 and 3,000K, occupied by candles, and incandescent (normal light bulbs) and tungsten (shop lights and many pro lighting fixtures) sources is slightly orange, and generally considered one of the "warm tones." At the other end of the spectrum is the bluish color produced by the blue sky, and generally considered one of the "cool tones." In between is the noon sun and "cool, white" fluorescent light bulbs.

The mere existence of this scale may surprise many readers. After all, our eyes see "white" irrespective of the color of the light. As it turns out, however, this is a case where our brain overrules our eyes. We see white paper, poster board, or other objects that we know are white, and our brain tells us they are white. Unfortunately, video cameras aren't that smart; you have to tell them what is white; and you do this when you set the camera's white balance.

Most video cameras have at least two white balance settings: one for outdoors, which assumes that the prevailing light is slightly bluish, and one for indoors, which assumes that the light is tinted slightly orange. In both instances, the camera corrects for the prevailing tint and makes white objects white.

In addition, most prosumer and all professional cameras have a manual white balance control; this obviously adds great flexibility when you're shooting somewhere between daylight and incandescent light—say, under cool, white fluorescent bulbs. However, if you have two light sources with conflicting color temperatures, white balance doesn't help, and the colors on some part of your image will be distorted.

Now, back to our scenarios. In the first scenario, you're mixing sunlight (5,600K) with an incandescent lamp (3,000K). If the white balance is set to indoors, the portion of the face lighted by the sun through the window will be blue. If it's set to outdoors, the portion of the face lighted by the indoor lamp will appear slightly orange.

The second scenario is more interesting. First, recognize that today's fluorescent bulbs have much more range color-wise, so just because you're using fluorescent lighting doesn't doom your subjects to a sickly green coloring. Second, while you can buy "cool white" fluorescents that produce light in the 4,000K range, you can also buy warmer lights that output close to the 2,700 to 3,000K produced by incandescent bulbs.

If the color output of your incandescent and fluorescent bulbs match, you've eliminated the white balance issue, and picture quality should be good. While color temperature values are seldom listed on a bulb's packaging, stores such as Lowe's often provide this information at the point of sale, and it's generally available on the manufacturer's Web site. I'll describe how to avoid problems in both scenarios in the Problem Solving section.

Application:

- Whenever you use different sources to light a scene, make sure the sources produce a consistent color temperature. Otherwise, your white balance will be incorrect for one or more sources, and distort your colors.

- When you're buying bulbs for your portable lighting gear, or for offices where you frequently shoot video, purchase bulbs that output similar color temperatures. If you're mixing incandescent with fluorescent bulbs, note that while there are fluorescent bulbs that match the color temperature of incandescent lighting, the reverse isn't true. If you have to mix, your only option is to buy fluorescents that match your incandescent.

The Color Rendering Index (CRI)

In addition to the color temperature of common lighting types, Figure 3.5 also shows the Color Rendering Index (CRI) of these lights. Briefly, CRI is a measure of how accurately the light portrays color, with 100 being ideal. Lights in the 60 to 65 range can make people and objects appear washed out, while lights in the 80 to 100 range bring out the colors.

The difference is too subtle to detect on the grayscale pages of this book, but General Electric has comparison shots posted at *www.gelighting.com/na/ institute/quality.html*. If you browse around the web site, you'll find it's a solid resource for additional information on lighting temperature and CRI. Scan the lighting racks at Lowe's or Web sites such as *www.bulbs.com* and you'll see that lights with higher CRIs cost a bit more. But in my experience they're well worth it.

Hard Versus Soft Lighting

Hard light is light transmitted from a lighting source in sharp, parallel rays that produce hard edges and dark, clearly defined shadows. Typically, hard light sources produce high quantities of light from a very compact space, accompanied by lots of heat, which causes problems in many environments.

The sun is a classic "hard light," as are unfrosted incandescent light bulbs and spotlights. In **Figure 3.6**, I used a hard light to produce the shot on the left. In addition to producing a slight shine on my forehead, the hard lighting produces significant contrast between the bright, right side of my face, and the left side, cast in dark shadows. This is the same effect we saw in the key light-only image in Figure 3.2. Without the fill light to minimize the shadows, details become lost in the darker regions of the frame.

Look at the effect the soft light has on the right in Figure 3.6. As you can see, it produces even lighting across my face and over the background, and minimal shadows. This makes soft light your only real choice for flat lighting, and for lighting backgrounds for chromakeying. (I'll explain chromakeying later.)

You can produce soft light (at least) three ways. First, you can use lights that are naturally softer, such as fluorescent lights. Second, you can "bounce" a hard light off of a light surface, such as a bounce card, which removes the hard edge, but typically requires either another person to hold the card or a dedicated stand.

Finally, you can install a diffuser, as shown on the left in **Figure 3.7**, over a hard light source, as shown on the right in the figure. I'll cover both bounce cards and diffusion kits in the upcoming Lighting Toolset section. For now, note that diffusers are pieces of cloth or other material that disperse the harsh light from a tungsten or incandescent source, converting hard light to soft light. In this instance, I used a cloth sheet from a Rosco diffusion kit that cost about $30 at Wolf Camera. Applied over one lamp of the $35 tungsten shop light I bought at Lowe's, it produces good, even lighting that can't be beat in terms of bang for the buck.

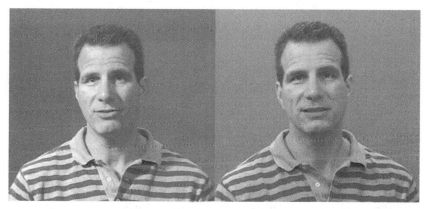

Figure 3.6. Hard lighting on the left creates contrast; soft lighting on the right is more even.

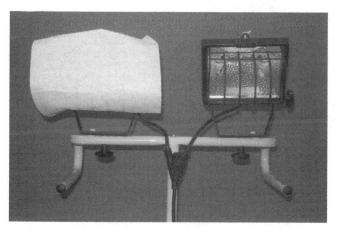

Figure 3.7.
Halogen shop lights with a diffusion sheet on the left.

Many television stations such as CNN are moving to fluorescent lights, which produce soft light and run much cooler than incandescent lights. The downside is that you need many more bulbs to create the same light as hard light sources such as the tungsten halogen lighting they are replacing. This makes fluorescent a great option for permanent studios, but less attractive for portable lighting. If you need to move your lights around, consider a hard light source such as tungsten or incandescent converted to soft light via a bounce card or diffuser.

Finally, while soft light is very flattering in many "people" shots; it can obscure detail in product or object-oriented shots. If you plan to shoot both objects and people, you'll probably need both hard and soft light sources.

Application:

- When planning your lighting, remember that soft lights are generally better for lighting faces and backgrounds than hard lights.

- Typically, hard lights are much more compact than soft lights, making them easier to carry and use. And, since you can easily convert hard light to soft light with diffusers or bounce cards, they make great additions to your lighting kit.

Defining "Good Lighting"

With this as background, let's briefly touch on what constitutes good lighting. In this regard, I find a quick review of Maslow's hierarchy very instructive.

Briefly, Maslow's hierarchy defines a range of human needs: from food, water, and sleep (physiological) to self-actualization. According to Maslow, human beings can't address higher-level needs until the more basic needs are satisfied.

Lighting has a similar hierarchy. It's lovely to consider how different lighting schemes can create moods or convey emotions, but in most business or academic shoots, our needs are much simpler.

Here is my hierarchy of good lighting:

First and most important, good lighting enables the camera to produce a high-quality image; though be careful not to overexpose the scene with too much light. Job Number 1 is to provide enough light so that critical scene elements can be clearly captured by the camera. Forget art, forget mood, and forget emotion.

Second, good lighting produces an image with reasonable contrast ratios. No areas should be so light or dark that detail is lost. Typically, if you have only one light, position it as a key light, but soften the light to minimize shadowing and contrast ratio. Alternatively, position a bounce card to catch light from the key light and serve as a fill light (see more on bounce cards in the Lighting Toolset section).

Third, good lighting has a consistent color temperature. When using multiple lights, their color temperatures should be close, if not identical.

Fourth, good lighting can be flat or three-point lighting, but in all cases should be back-lighted.

Fifth, when shooting one subject under ideal conditions, go for three-point lighting (OK, so I'm a snob). When shooting multiple subjects, three-point lighting is very complicated—even in studio conditions—so go with flat lighting.

The Lighting Toolset

Now, let's examine the tools at our disposal to help produce good lighting.

Sources of Light

Unless you're buying exotic professional lighting gear, your choice of bulb and fixture is limited to incandescent, quartz-halogen, and fluorescent. Let's briefly discuss each type.

Incandescent Bulbs

There are the common household light bulbs that screw into most lamps and light fixtures. Incandescent bulbs are also called tungsten bulbs because they use a tungsten filament; this is the element that glows and creates brightness or light glows when heated with electricity. Unlike fluorescent lights, incandescent bulbs run very hot, which contributes to their short life (750 to 1,000 hours). When the light burns out, the filament breaks into small chunks, creating the noise you hear when you shake the bulb. Some incandescent bulbs use heavy-duty filaments or different gases-side in the bulb, which can give you four times the longevity.

Benefits and Effects

Incandescent bulbs give off a hard, yellowish light—typically referred to as "warm" —and have a very high CRI of 95. Overall, these bulbs are convenient because they're available in most offices and homes, but when they're your primary light source, be sure to white balance your camera accordingly.

Halogen Bulbs

These bulbs are also called quartz-halogen or tungsten-halogen (as shown in Figure 3.2). Basically, halogen bulbs use a tungsten filament like standard incandescent bulbs, but halogen gas in the bulb helps preserve the filament and boost the bulb's lifespan. These bulbs burn at more than 480 degrees Fahrenheit, which is too hot for a standard glass bulb, so they either require a quartz bulb (hence, the name quartz-halogen) or a special heat-resistant glass bulb.

These bulbs burn so hot manufacturers recommend installing them with gloves as the skin's oil on the bulb can cause premature failure. The intense heat also makes halogen bulbs more of a fire hazard than incandescent bulbs, so be careful when using them around curtains, table cloths, or similarly flammable materials.

Benefits and Effects

Halogen bulbs are generally more powerful than standard incandescent bulbs, which max out at about 100 watts. Halogens can be as powerful as 1,000 watts (120 volt) or 1,600 watts (240 volt). The ability to produce this power from a relatively small fixture makes halogen extremely efficient when you need lots of light, though you'll need a special fixture such as the shop light shown in Figure 3.7 to use higher-powered halogen bulbs.

Halogen bulbs produce a hard light that is whiter and purer than incandescent bulbs, but shares the same high CRI.

Fluorescent Bulbs

Fluorescent bulbs run an electric current through a tube filled with argon and mercury gases; this combination produces ultraviolet radiation, and activates a phosphorous coating in the bulb to produce light. Fluorescents run cooler than incandescents or halogens, and last much longer.

You can purchase fluorescent bulbs with a variety of color temperatures: from "daylight" bulbs that mimic the color temperature of the sun to 3,000K bulbs that are close to incandescent bulbs—the CRI varying significantly from bulb to bulb.

Benefits and Effects

Compact fluorescent bulbs fit into a standard lamp fixture, making them easier to use in the office and the home.

All fluorescents output a soft light that is great for flat lighting, or serving as a fill light, but probably not sufficiently focused for key lights.

Camera-Mounted Lights

Most camera-mounted lights tend to be halogen bulbs. They produce a hard light that frequently engenders a deer-in-the-headlights look and is definitely hard on the subject's eyes. When a person is facing the camera, camera-mounted lights produce very flat lighting with no back light, which can create a very unattractive effect on the person being filmed.

Benefits and Effects

These lights are invaluable when shooting night or during parties and receptions, but are best used only when no alternative is available.

Bounce Cards (Reflector Boards)

Bounce card is the generic name for any surface that can reflect light from a direct light source—typically to serve as a fill light as shown in **Figure 3.8**. As discussed above, bounce cards are also effective for bouncing light up from a lap or table to fill facial shadows.

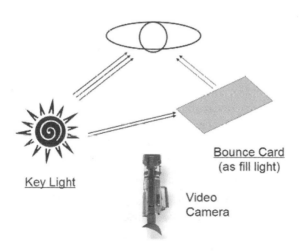

Figure 3.8.
Use a bounce card as fill light by reflecting light from a strong, hard source.

Key Light

Bounce Card
(as fill light)

Video
Camera

For casual use, a simple whiteboard from an arts & crafts store—or any hard white object for that matter—will work just fine. For heavy use, especially on the road, consider purchasing a professional reflector that you can fold up for easy storage. Professional reflectors, which generally cost less than $100, often have different colors on each side like white for sunlight and gold for sunset. Photoflex is a very popular manufacturer of reflector boards; check out their offerings at *www.photoflex.com*.

Diffusion Kits

Diffusion kits contain packets of cloth and other materials that change the character of the light produced by your light fixture. Some variations are artistic, but the ones I find most valuable are those that convert hard light to soft light by diffusing the beam from the source light.

The Rosco kit I mentioned earlier has proven durable, easy to attach to my homegrown lighting kit, and heat-resistant—even when used on 500-watt halogen bulbs. Essentially, the kit enables every light in my kit to provide both hard and soft light, making the $30 I spent well worth the investment.

As a quick aside, some authors report using fabric-softener sheets to diffuse their light beams, but only after several drying cycles to eliminate the smell. As with all diffusion materials, you can't place them directly on the glass—especially when stronger halogens are used—because they can catch fire.

Read more about diffusion materials and what's inside the Rosco kit at *www.rosco.com/main.html.*

Gels (Filters)

Gels are the plastic films placed in front of a light to change its characteristics. For example, if you were using the sun as the key light and needed a fill light to match its color, you would place a blue gel over a halogen or incandescent bulb to make it match the sun.

Conversely, if you needed the sunlight streaming into the room to match the halogen lighting in the scene, you would place an orange or straw-colored gel over the window. Similarly, if bright light streaming in from a window produced too much backlighting, you could apply a neutral-density gel to reduce the light's intensity without changing the color.

To be honest, I've not worked that much with gels, primarily because rolls of gel suitable for covering windows are expensive, and the brittle gel sheets are tough to attach to my ad hoc lighting gear. For indoor shooting, it's easier for me to match the color of my fluorescent and halogen bulbs.

You can download the excellent Rosco Guide to Color Filters from the Technotes section of the company's Web site (*www.rosco.com/main.html*).

Lenses

You can also use lenses attached to the camera (or in some cases, embedded in the camera) to help control lighting. For example, Neutral Density filters (also called ND filters or gray filters) reduce the amount of light entering your camera, but don't change the color temperature. This gives much greater flexibility when working in direct sunlight, as shown in **Figure 3.9**.

The image on the left shows the Sony VX2000 shooting with the ND filter disabled; as you can see, the video is so bright it's unusable. The middle figure shows the ND filter set to 1, while the figure on the right shows the ND filter set to 2.

Note that the results produced by ND filters will vary depending on what shooting mode you're in. For example, in Figure 3.9, I'm in "aperture priority mode" (where I set the aperture manually), which prevents the camera from automatically adjusting the aperture to minimize the impact of the brightness. This maximizes the effect of the filter, which is what I was intending to show.

Figure 3.9. The Sony VX2000 has a two-step neutral-density filter to help tame direct sunlight.

In fully automatic shooting modes, the filter allows the camera to shoot much clearer images, because it lets the camera eliminate what the Sony manual calls "diffraction off the small aperture" shown in **Figure 3.10**. Whatever mode I'm in, my VX2000 blinks to tell me whether I should engage the ND filter and at which value—a tremendous advantage over nonintegrated filters screwed onto the end of the lens. Whatever your filter/camera combination, you should experiment with the ND filter in *all* shooting modes before using it on a real shoot.

Popular lens manufacturers, Tiffen, discusses ND filters on its Web site: *www.tiffen.com/NEUTRAL%20DENSITY.htm.*

Figure 3.10. In automatic exposure mode, the neutral-density filter increases sharpness, though your mileage may vary.

Zebra Pattern

This is a camcorder feature rather than a true accessory, but a great tool for shooting inside and out. Briefly, as you can see in **Figure 3.11**, the camcorder shows a zebra pattern on certain parts of the image when it is overexposed. Using my VX2000, I can set this feature to 70 IRE, which shows whether the video is appropriately exposed for Caucasian skin tones, or to 100 IRE, which is pure white, or too "hot" for NTSC viewing. In Figure 3.11, the zebra pattern is set to 100 IRE. At this setting, the video will be way overexposed, as you can see from the image on the left in Figure 3.9.

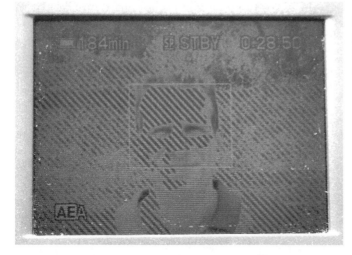

Figure 3.11.
A zebra pattern lets you know when the image is overexposed.

Just for the record, IRE stands for Institute of Radio Engineers, the folks who originally defined these video signal values.

User Scenarios

Now that we've run through the basics and the tools, let's review some common user scenarios, starting with the two situations mentioned in All Lights Have a Different Color Temperature on page 41. To save you a flipping back, I'll recap them here.

Situation 1: You're shooting indoors, using sunlight streaming in from a window as your key light, and a lamp in the room as a fill light.

Options:

- Shut the curtains and use indoor lighting exclusively.

- Switch off the indoor lighting and use a bounce card to reflect the sunlight from the window as a fill light (see Figure 3.8). Framing has to be tight using this alternative, because the card has to be close to the subject, and you'll either need a stand or an assistant to hold the bounce card.

- Use a fluorescent light with a daylight fluorescent bulb to match the color temperature of the sunlight.

- Use an orange or straw-colored gel film to convert the incoming sunlight to incandescent levels.

Situation 2: You're shooting indoors, lighting the scene primarily with fluorescent lights in the office ceiling, and using an incandescent lamp to reduce facial shadows.

Options:

- Use 3,000K fluorescent lights in the office ceiling.

- Use a compact fluorescent bulb in the lamp to match the color temperature of the ceiling fluorescents.

- Gel the incandescent lamp to match the color temperature of the ceiling fluorescents.

Situation 3: Your subject is wearing glasses.

Options:

- Ask the subject to remove her glasses.

- Use soft key and fill lights and position them to the side of the subject, as shown in **Figure 3.12**.

Figure 3.12.
When your subject won't take off her glasses, position soft lights on either side, and in addition to the back light.

Situation 4: Your subject wants to be shot against a window during daylight.

Options:

• Shoot early morning or late afternoon when the sun is weakest.

• Use Gel rolls to cover the window to reduce the incoming light.

Situation 5: You have to shoot a subject in an office lighted by fluorescent lights.

Options:

• I've used the setup shown in **Figure 3.13** to good effect, though the lighting is flat. Position the subject slightly in front of one light, which then serves as the back light, with the other light serving as the sole key light. If shadowing is a problem, position a small fluorescent desk lamp *upwards at* the subject's face, or use a bounce card.

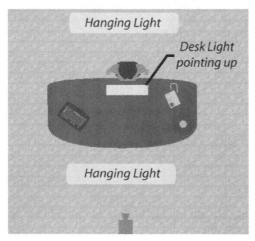

Figure 3.13.
When shooting in an office with fluorescent lights, position the subject between the overheads and use a bounce card or small fluorescent light pointing upwards to remove facial shadows.

Situation 6: You're shooting in a home or office where lamps provide the only available lighting.

Options:

- My approach here is simple: move the lights and lamps into the desired three-point positioning, removing the covers if possible, to achieve the best lighting. Look at the example shown in **Figure 3.14** from the interview scenario, where floor lamps are moved into key and fill position. I usually carry clamp lights like that shown on the right in **Figure 3.15** for hanging from curtain rods, chandeliers, or any other fixed item that gives me the positioning I need.

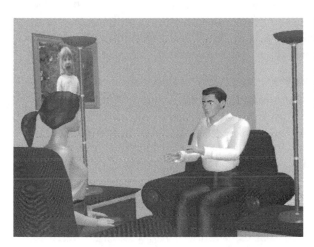

Figure 3.14.
Going native: When shooting without your lighting kit, don't be afraid to move lamps into the key, fill, and back light positions to achieve the necessary lighting.

Figure 3.15.
Rosco's Diffusion Kit and Incandescent Clamp Light—the finest in guerilla lighting.

Professional Versus Homegrown Lighting

If you compared the bulb from the shop lamp in Figure 3.7 to the bulb in a professional lighting kit—say, the Lowel Tota-Light—you would find minimal differences, though the Tota-Light, *without* stand, retails at about $170. To replace my $35 shop lamp with Lowel equipment I'd need to invest more than $300, and I'd still need to find stands. Or, I could spend $1,000-plus and get a four-light Lowel system with all the accessories.

On its face, this may sound excessive. But it's worth noting that the Lowel system comes with a convenient carrying case that simplifies shooting on the go. The Lowel gear also has "barn doors" and other accessories that simplify directing the light, and convenient clamps and knobs for attaching umbrella reflectors and hoods. And rather than using paper clips and other ad hoc connectors to attach your diffusion materials to the lamp, you'll use a convenient stand. This all translates to convenience, time savings, and equipment durability.

The truth is, I salivate over these types of lighting rigs and if I were a full-time videographer, I'd definitely buy one. However, for the type of intermittent shooting I do, I can get by with much cheaper equipment. Though my homegrown kit won't look as impressive to my customers as the branded gear, generally they care more about the quality of the video; if I'm careful, the customer won't know (or care) whether I used Lowel gear or a shop lamp from Lowe's.

Two other pieces of lighting gear I couldn't live without are shown in Figure 3.15. The Rosco Diffusion Kit easily converts my halogen lamps to soft lights (for around $35), and the work lamp (right) with its own steel clamp, is marvelous for connecting to doors, lights, shelves, windows, cabinets, and pretty much everything else I've tried attaching it to. These clamp lights cost less than $10 and take both incandescent and compact fluorescent bulbs, providing great flexibility when attempting to match office lighting.

Bruce A. Johnson's "Lighting on the Cheap," originally published in *DV Magazine* (*www.dv.com/print_me.jhtml?LookupId=/xml/feature/2001/bjohnson0401*), and "Creating a Low-Cost Fluorescent Lighting System" from Studio 1 Productions (*www.studio1productions.com/Articles/FL-Lights.htm*) both offer great advice on creating low-cost lighting systems.

Chapter 4:
Digital Production Workflows

OK, we've shot our video, captured great audio, and now we're ready to transfer the video to our computer and start editing. Before getting started, let's take a high-level look at the process and define some key terms and concepts. That way, you'll be ready when the talk starts getting technical.

DV Production Workflow—Definitions

Take a look at the illustration below; it illustrates digital video production workflow from camera to output. Some of the terms may be new, so I'll start by defining the key terms.

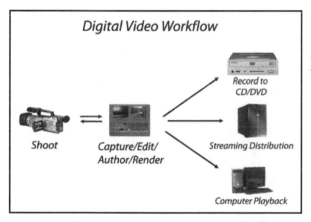

Figure 4.1.
The digital video workflow: from camera to distribution (and back to camera).

- *Capturing*—This is the process of transferring video from camera to computer. If you're working with a DV camcorder, this is much like transferring a file from one computer to another: quick, easy, and all-digital, except that it happens in real time (e.g., while it is playing which is considerably slower than what we've come to expect from file transfers). In contrast, when capturing from an analog camcorder (like VHS or Hi8), the computer or capture device first converts the analog audio and video to a digital format (known as "digitizing"), then compresses the audio and video to fit more on your hard drive.

- *Editing*—Editing is the process of preparing captured video for viewing. Typically, this involves cutting away extraneous footage, reordering sequences, and adding titles and transitions. If you shot noddies or cutaways as described in Chapter 1, this also involves piecing the various clips into a watchable whole. When we speak of editing in a digital context, we're talking about nonlinear editing; unlike old-school, dual-deck analog video editing, with nonlinear digital video editing on computers, we can easily resequence our footage as we choose.

- *Authoring*—Authoring is a key step in creating DVDs—the step that distinguishes DVDs from other just-the-movie media. It's the process of creating menus, linking them to content such as video and slideshows, encoding the video (see below), and recording the result to a DVD recorder. Though you can burn any video file to a DVD using a variety of software programs, unless you use an dedicated authoring program, such as iDVD the disc will not play on a consumer DVD player.

- *Rendering*—All the editing you do in your video editor is "nondestructive," which means the video you captured to your hard drive is never modified by your video editing software. Instead, the software provides a visual workspace for trimming videos, sequencing trimmed clips, editing and adjusting audio, and adding titles, transitions, effects, and the like. When you're done, the editor creates a new file (working from the captured videos and your various edit instructions), and encodes it into the format and data rate you requested. This final process, which encompasses not just format encoding but processing effects, is called rendering.

- *Writing to tape*—In Figure 4.1, you'll notice there are two arrows between the camcorder and the software icon. The arrow pointing from the camera to the editing screen is the capture process, while the arrow returning to the DV camera carries the final edited video back to the camera—a process called "writing to tape." Once the video is stored on tape, you can use the camera's analog video outputs (the ones you use to connect your camera to a television set) to "copy" the edited video to a VHS tapeor other analog format. You will need this type of output, if you have a conference room, classroom, or customer using a VHS deck rather than a DVD player or computer.

Note that your workflow will vary depending on what products you use to edit and author your video. For example, some programs can do it all: capture, edit, author, and burn to DVD. Others only operate as video editors and require a separate program for authoring. Both approaches have their virtues; for the purposes of this chapter, consider them identical.

These are the definitions; now let's jump into the workflow itself. As most readers will be working with DV camcorders, let's examine what the DV in digital video actually is.

DV—Our Starting Point

All video you watch on your computer is digital, but not all digital video is DV. Specifically, unlike analog camcorders, DV camcorders convert information captured thought the lens as digital data. The compression technology (or codec) used is the DV codec; a standard technology mutually adapted by the camera and computer communities.

You don't have to do anything special to make the camera capture the video in DV format, it just does, and the computers that download the files from the camera know this and handle the format automatically. If all you're doing is capturing video, editing on the computer and sending the video back to the camera or creating DVDs, most of the workflow and file details covered here are also handled automatically, and this chapter provides information you really don't need to get your work done.

On the other hand, if you'll be compressing your video into formats like Windows Media, RealVideo or QuickTime, you need to understand the basics covered in this section. I'll cover some specifics about compression in About Compression, the next major section. Although DV stands for digital video, it's a specific digital video format. There are many digital video codecs, but only one is properly called DV.

Figure 4.2 shows the file information window from a video editor—the DV file in this example is in AVI format, which stands for Audio/Video Interleaved, and means the file is stored in Microsoft's "Video for Windows" format. Briefly, a file format is essentially a specification for how information is stored in that file. If a file conforms to a particular standard, any application that also conforms to that standard can open and edit the file. Thus any Video-for-Windows-compatible video editor can edit any AVI file, just as any QuickTime-compatible video editor can edit any MOV file, the standard for Mac users.

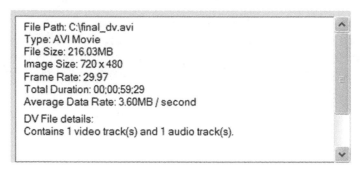

File Path: C:\final_dv.avi
Type: AVI Movie
File Size: 216.03MB
Image Size: 720 x 480
Frame Rate: 29.97
Total Duration: 00;00;59;29
Average Data Rate: 3.60MB / second

DV File details:
Contains 1 video track(s) and 1 audio track(s).

Figure 4.2. DV file details from the information screen of a video editor.

Formats and Codecs

Note the distinction between format and compression technology, or codec (which stands for compression/decompression) The specifications for audio/video compression technologies also include information on how to *de*compress video compressed in that format. Codecs are technologies that compress video during capture or for delivery. For example, as mentioned above, DV is a codec. When you capture digital video from a camcorder on the Mac, you capture into MOV format, but the compression technology is still DV. When you capture DV video on a Windows computer, you capture into AVI format.

The key point here is that format and compression technology are not the same thing. A QuickTime file can be compressed with a DV codec, the Sorenson codec, the MPEG-4 codec, and several legacy codecs such as Cinepak and Indeo. The same goes for the Video for Windows format. Often when you're producing a file for final distribution, you'll make separate decisions about what format you use to output the file and what codec you use to compress the file. So, it's critical to realize that they are not identical concepts.

In Figure 4.2, the next parameter after Type is File Size. Though the example file is only about 1 minute long (total duration, 00:00:59.29), the captured file is 216MB in size. Size isn't an issue for DV cameras, which use tapes that can store up to 120 minutes of video. Since 120 minutes of digital video takes up 26GB on your hard drive, the size of your digital video is more of an issue during editing, though not a show stopper given that 200GB disk drives now cost less than $250.

That said, if you tried to send that same video file to a remote viewer over a modem, it would take roughly forever. While DV is great for capturing great quality with your camcorder, you'll need to choose a more compact codec than the one built into your camcorder to deliver the final edited video to your viewers.

The next parameter is Image Size, often called resolution, which is the width and height of the pixels in each frame of the video. All digital video files consist of pixels; digital video files are always 720 pixels across and 480 pixels high (720x480), which is the size of the larger image in **Figure 4.3**. Sometimes you'll render video at 720x480 resolution, most notably when producing for DVD or computer-based playback. However, if you're producing a streaming file for viewing over the Internet, you'll render the file at a smaller resolution, such as 320x240, also called quarter-screen video (see inset, Figure 4.3).

The next parameter in the file information screen is Frame Rate, listed as 29.97 frames per second (fps); this means that during normal playback, 29.97 frames display each second. This frame rate is compliant with NTSC, the broadcast standard for video transmitted over North American televisions. When producing for DVD or hard-disk playback, you'll render your video files at this frame rate. However, when producing video for the internet, you'll reduce the frame rate to around 15fps or below.

When you render at 15fps, the editor will exclude (or drop) every other frame in the video from the rendered file. During playback, over the same one-second period, the viewer will see 15 frames, not 29.97, which can look a bit choppy during high-action sequences, but is undetectable for most talking-head videos.

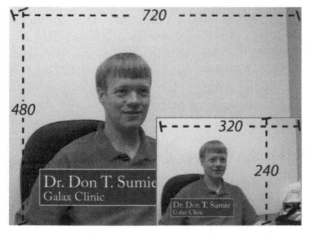

Figure 4.3.
Full-screen (720x480) and quarter-screen (320x240) video.

The next parameter, Total Duration, is 59 seconds, 29 frames, just a hair under one full minute. As in Figure 4.3, duration is always displayed in hours:minutes:second.frames.

Finally, there's Data Rate, which defines the amount of data associated with each second of video. As you can see, the data rate for digital video is 3.6 megabytes per second (MB/sec).

So, what are the key takeaways?

1. Get familiar with the starting point for all of your video production efforts. No file you produce will have a greater resolution than 720x480, a faster frame rate than 29.97fps, or a larger data rate than 3.6MB/sec.

2. Understand that all digital files are defined by the same set of parameters. The file documented in Figure 4.3 is in Windows Media *format*, encoded with a *compression codec*, at a *resolution* of 720x480 pixels, a *frame rate* of 29.97 frames per second, and a *data rate* of 3.6 megabytes per second. Once you learn these file parameters, you know everything you need to know about a digital video file.

About Compression

For practical purposes, all digital video files are compressed; otherwise you would not be able to fit them on your hard disk or play them on your computer. Even DV video is compressed, though much less so than most other compressed formats.

You're probably familiar with a range of compression technologies, including MPEG, RealVideo, Sorenson, and Windows Media Video. Note that RealVideo and Windows Media are also formats with their own file extension, .RM for RealMedia, .WMV for Windows Media Video. MPEG is also a format, and MPEG-1 and -2 files use an .MPG or similar extension, though MPEG-4 is a broader technology that plays under multiple formats, including MPEG, QuickTime, and Windows Media. Sorenson is a pure codec that encodes into the QuickTime format.

All video compression technologies are "lossy," which means they encode by throwing away the original pixel-related information and using complex algorithms to store a facsimile of the original file. Compression works in a number of ways; the simplest example is a talking-head video with an unchanging background. In the original, uncompressed video, that background requires as many bits of information in each frame as other parts of the frame where there's movement. A compression algorithm will store information describing the background once, and then eliminate this redundant information in subsequent frames, which is very efficient. In higher-motion videos, such as football games or action movies, there is very little redundancy between frames, making these videos much harder to compress. With all lossy technologies, the more you compress, the more you lose, and the more degraded the quality of the video. Conversely, all things being equal, the higher the data rate, the higher the video quality.

Produce a 500Kbps file with any codec, and it will probably look pretty good. Use the same codec to compress the same source video at 10Kbps, and it will probably look pretty awful. This doesn't mean that the technology is in any way faulty; it's just a fact of life about compression.

What are the key takeaways?

- There are a number of video cameras now shipping that encode video in MPEG-2 or MPEG-4 formats, usually at a data rate of 1.2MB/sec—one third that of DV—or lower. These cameras offer great value-adds, such as the ability to produce a DVD on-the-fly that you can watch on your TV set (they shoot directly to mini-DVD discs instead of mini-DV tapes).

- However, at one third the data rate of DV video, at best, the quality captured by these cameras suffers. Sometimes it's subtle, sometimes unnoticeable, but in the $4,000 and below price range, the DV codec in a DV camera is the best available acquisition codec, or the best compression technology to use when shooting a video.

- Since DV video, at 3.6MB/sec, is simply too large to distribute in any media, you'll have to render the finished video into a delivery codec, perhaps MPEG-2, perhaps MPEG-4, or some other, to distribute the video to your viewers. Keep in mind the distinction between acquisition and delivery codes; the optimal video workflow shoots and captures in the highest-quality acquisition codec—usually DV—and outputs in the highest-quality delivery codec that meets the target data rate and other distribution parameters. Any other workflow is suboptimal.

- Each time you encode a file, you degrade the quality, much like photocopying a photocopy. The optimal workflow is to capture in digital video and stay in DV until you finally output for distribution.

Now let's tackle the most important concept in digital video distribution.

It's All About the Bandwidth

At a high level, bandwidth defines the ability of a system or subsystem to transfer data. For example, a 56.6Kbps modem has a bandwidth of 56.6Kbps, and can transfer up to 56.6 kilobits per second from the Internet into your computer. Most of the time, access to fast and consistent bandwidth isn't an issue. For example, when checking your email or surfing the Web, a delay of a second or two here and there can go unnoticed.

However, video is a real-time event with a synchronized audiovisual stream. Once playback starts, if the computer can't access the video stream fast enough, the video slows, stops, or sometimes drops quality. For example, if you connect to the Internet via a 56.6Kbps modem, and start playing a 300Kbps stream from ESPN or CNN, the video will quickly stop playing. Why? Because the data rate of the video file exceeds the bandwidth capacity of your modem. The data stream is bigger than the pipe.

Our job as video producers is to produce video files, especially when producing streaming video with a data rate smaller than the bandwidth capacity of the viewers who will watch them.

Keep one thought in mind as you walk down this video production road: the quality of the video you produce is directly related to the bandwidth of the medium used to distribute it. DVD players have a very high bandwidth, so DVD-Video looks great. However, if you're required to stream video to folks connecting to the Internet at 56Kbps or below, the video will look substantially worse.

This disparity in quality, of course, has nothing to do with your skills as a video producer; rather, it's all about the bandwidth. It's a simple enough concept—just make sure the person who's judging the quality of your work, be it spouse, boss, parent, or child, understands it as well. And under no circumstances, commit to the quality of video you can deliver until you know which medium you'll use to distribute it.

About Bits and Bytes

Bandwidth and data rate play a vital role in the quality of your video, so let's take a closer look at how they are measured. The bit-byte breakdown is shown in **Table 4.1**.

When I first started working with video, the most important bandwidth measure was the data transfer speed of a CD-ROM, which started at 150 kilobytes per second, a so-called "1X" drive. Today, CD-ROMs can retrieve and transfer data at 48X and higher, or 7.2 megabytes of information per second, which makes the 1X drive seem glacial.

Table 4.1.

	Bits	Bytes
56 kbps modem	56 kbps	7 KB/s
Single speed CD-ROM	1200 kbps	150 KB/s
Single speed DVD	10800 kbps	1350 KB/s
DSL/cable	512 kbps	64 KB/s
T-1	1540 kbps	192.5 KB/s

However, as shown in Table 4.1, many video producers are surprised to learn that the bandwidth of a single-speed CD-ROM drive (150 KB/s) is almost as fast as a T1 line (192.5 KB/s) that costs hundreds of dollars a month. Briefly, to convert bits to bytes, you divide by 8, so the 1540 kilobits per second throughput of T-1 converts to 192.5 kilobytes per second. Conversely, to get from bytes to bits, you multiply by 8, which is how a single speed CD-ROM converts from 150 kilobytes per second to 1200 kilobits per second.

With a 56K modem, admittedly slow, but still a very pervasive method of connecting to the Internet, you have a throughput of only 7 kilobytes per second, roughly 1/20th the transfer speed of a long obsolete single speed CD-ROM drive.

That's pretty sobering. Even a relatively fast DSL connection of 512 kilobits per second translates to only 64 kilobytes per second, about two-thirds the speed of a 1X CD-ROM. If you're wondering why video streaming over the Internet generally looks so bad, that's your answer.

Before we delve too deeply into bandwidth and data rate speeds, it's important to note that over the years, most encoding tools have evolved from talking in bytes per second to bits per second. In this book, I'll use Kbps and Mbps to connote kilobits and megabits per second, and KB/sec and MB/sec to connote kilobytes and megabytes per second. Most production tools have transitioned over from bytes to bits, so when I mention a data rate or bandwidth capacity, it will generally be in bits, not bytes.

Choosing Your Delivery Codec

I've said that DV is the optimal acquisition codec, I'm sure you're wondering about the best delivery codec. I'll briefly touch on the rules I follow here, and discuss them more thoroughly in Chapter 7 when we actually render some video:

* *DVD production*—DVDs require MPEG-2 video. Most editing and authoring tools have presets that make choosing compression options one-button simple; I almost always use these presets as well.

* *Computer hard drive playback*—I use Windows Media for almost all desktop playback.

* *Streaming*—Typically, your choice here is determined by the choice of streaming media server used by your organization, or a preference from the Web site czar. Beyond this, I typically use Windows Media as well, primarily because it's easier to integrate into FrontPage, which is the authoring program I use for my Web work.

For a comprehensive quality comparison of Windows Media, Real, MPEG-2, Sorenson (the technology used for QuickTime movie trailers), and MPEG-4, check out *www.emedialive.com/Articles/PrintArticle.aspx?ArticleID=8422.*

Chapter 5:
Editing Techniques

We've shot our video, now it's time to capture and edit it into final form. Though many detailed books have been written on video editing, we can break it down into a seven-step process and cover the most important points in a single chapter—when you're producing for business or educational use, the editing is typically focused and simple.

Of our three scenarios—executive briefing, group discussion, and interview—the interview is clearly the most complex from an editing perspective; you'll be weaving multiple sources of video, interview footage, cutaways, and noddies into one video. For this reason, I'll use interview footage to demonstrate the points made in this chapter.

I'll start by describing how to split, trim, sequence, and integrate your clips into a cohesive video; these in my view are among the most important tasks we discuss in this book. I'll describe how to create titles and credits, covering issues such as where to put your titles, which fonts to use, and how to make them legible when streaming at low bitrates. Then I'll discuss still-image overlay, including how to add your logo or watermark to the video, and conclude with a quick look at fading in and out of your video.

Admittedly each video is different and requires customized fine tuning. However, the steps outlined here probably account for 90 to 95percent of your editing efforts on each project, and should get you a long way towards completion.

1. Getting Started

Basically, there are two types of projects: those with time limitations (the duration of the video), and those without. Working without time limits is certainly easier; you lay out all of your footage, add the necessary garnish (titles, fades, logos), and render your project.

Of course, even if your project has no stated time limit, often sheer watchability imposes its own limitations. If you want audiences to enjoy watching your video, you'll need to remove the extraneous to highlight the relevant. Obviously, when your project has a strict time limit—whether it's two, five, or ten minutes— identifying what to leave in and out is, without question, the most important editing function.

So before you start editing, identify the target duration for the project. Then it's time to capture or import your video into your video editor, and begin massaging it into shape.

First, let's take care of a couple housekeeping issues.

*   Most video editors have an auto save function that saves a project at a specified interval. Find this function in your editor (search the help files for Auto Save or Save), make sure the feature is active, and set it to a reasonable interval, such as five or ten minutes is usual. That way, if your computer crashes mid-edit, your losses are limited.

*   Put together a file storage strategy. I create a separate folder on my capture drive for each project, and configure my editor to capture and write all temporary files created during editing to that folder. That way, I'll know where to find the files to delete or reuse after the project is done. On the Windows front, most editors default to Windows XP's My Documents folder for file storage, often making files nearly impossible to find. So, find a Preferences, Options, or Setup dialog in your editing program, pick a folder or file path, and make sure you know where your files are going.

2. Capture Your Video

Video capture procedures are program-specific and generally well covered in product manuals or help files, so I'll defer to those materials. My only caveat: make sure you capture with "scene detection" enabled.

Part of the information stored on the DV tape is the start point and stop point of each shot taken with the camcorder. During capture, video editing tools use this information to "detect scenes" and create separate clips for each time you started and stopped the camera. In my project, this won't break up the interview footage into separate clips as it was shot without turning the camera on or off, but the editor does place most of my cutaways, establishing shots, and noddies into separate clips, which are then easy to identify and use. I always capture with scene-detection enabled—usually a single-click selection in your editor's capture preferences (though you may have to set scene-detection "sensitivity," too).

After capture, all video editors insert the captured clips into some kind of library (also called bin or collection), which generally opens automatically when you close the capture window and switch to edit mode. However, capabilities and features differ substantially from program to program, as I'll discuss in the next section.

3. Finalize Your Audio Track

Editing styles differ, and there's no right or wrong way to start. However, when I'm editing, my first goal is to finalize my audio track. This means identifying all clips containing audio I want to include in the final video—usually interview footage, noddies, and some B-Roll—and inserting them into the project. This will create a complete and final audio track that will run throughout the project, regardless of the video that may accompany it at any given time. After the audio track is set, I'll insert noddies without audio, cutaways, and establishing shots, then work on logos and titles.

How I categorize and isolate clips from the captured video depends on the program I'm using. Many programs allow you to split clips up in the library (or wherever the captured video is stored), which simplifies the process of identifying keeper clips and discarding the rest. **Figure 5.1**, a screen shot from Microsoft's Movie Maker 2, illustrates this.

Figure 5.1.
Microsoft's Movie Maker in Storyboard view. Note the video assets in the "Collection" on the upper left, which I've already cut into discrete usable chunks, and the storyboard on the bottom, where I sequence my clips.

The upper left window displays the library (called Collection in Movie Maker and Album in other programs) containing my project video. After capture, I split all captured video into the smallest usable chunks, for example cutting each response from the physician into a separate segment. You probably can't read the descriptive names in Figure 5.1, but I created separate clips for the doctor's explanation of the challenges of his practice, describing his diverse client base, and the like. I also split the cutaways, questions, and noddies into separate clips the same way.

Most programs have a "split" or "razor" tool for scene-splitting; with Movie Maker, it's the "razor" icon on the left beneath the monitor window in the upper right. To split a video in the album, you touch the video with your cursor, which makes it appear in the monitor window, use the playback controls to move to the frame where you'd like to split the video, and then click the icon. The program will then create a new clip containing the second portion of the original clip, and display it in the album.

After splitting the clips, I drag them down to the storyboard—the sequential presentation of clips on the bottom half of Figure 5.1. Not all programs have a storyboard, but when they do, it's a great place to sequence your videos into the proper order. Generally, you move the videos into the storyboard window, where you can move them around like checkers on a checkerboard.

Once I've imported all the clips into the project, I'll switch to Timeline view, shown in **Figure 5.2**, for further editing. Where the storyboard shows each clip as the same size, irrespective of duration, the timeline is a time-based graphical representation of the project, with the length of the clip shown on the screen proportional to its actual duration in the project. The squiggly lines beneath the video clips are audio waveforms, a graphical representation of the audio shot with the video, while other "tracks" or layers in the timeline are available to add background audio, transitions, and titles.

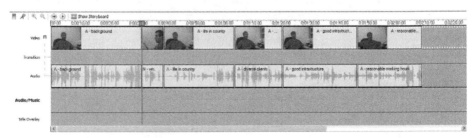

Figure 5.2. Movie Maker in Timeline view.

In Timeline view I'll trim the video, removing unwanted frames from the front and back of a clip. When I split clips in the album, I'm not trying to be precise; I'm just isolating all the videos I'll include in the project. Once in the timeline, I'll trim the videos, front and back once again, until only the desired footage is included.

Virtually all programs trim the same way: you touch the clip, hover your cursor over the edge you want to adjust, then grab and drag the edge to the desired location. Typically, as you drag the edge of the video, the monitor will display the then-current frame to assist your positioning.

Note that many prosumer tools don't allow you to split clips in the clip library, or create a storyboard, so you have to do all this work on the timeline. When editing with these tools, I drag the primary video (in this case the interview footage) down to the timeline, and split and trim the video into the final chunks there.

Generally, splitting on the timeline is similar to splitting in the album. You use playback controls to locate the edit line (see **Figure 5.3**) to the desired split position, and then click on the razor icon or similar tool. The video will split into two clips, each of which you can trim separately, or delete for that matter. As virtually all editors are "non-destructive," you can delete clips in the album or timeline without actually deleting the captured video.

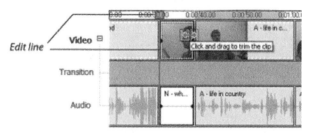

Figure 5.3.
To trim a clip in most programs, simply grab and drag the edge, as shown here in Movie Maker.

4.   Add Cutaways, Noddies, and Establishing Shots

Once you'v assembled all the clips that contribute audio to the project on the timeline, it's time to start adding other shots. Before we get to this, let's look at some of the goals to consider while editing.

Avoid Jump Cuts

Take another look at Figure 5.2. Remember that I've trimmed all the clips of the doctor to remove unwanted frames from the beginning and end, so the clips don't flow smoothly from one to the other. For this reason, when the video moves from one clip to another, it's likely the image will jump from the frame shown on the left in **Figure 5.4** to the frame shown on the right.

This is called a "jump cut," because the video looks like it's jumping around. One moment viewers are watching the doctor with his hands on the chair, and the next moment they're seeing his arms waving in the air. Jump cuts are very disconcerting to the viewer because they make no visual sense.

And, they create a problem any time you edit video of a relatively static scene and subject shot with a fixed camera. Fortunately, jump cuts are easy to avoid, if you take the time to shoot cutaways or noddies. This is illustrated in **Figure 5.5**.

Figure 5.4. A "jump cut" showing the last frame of the fifth video and the first frame of the sixth.

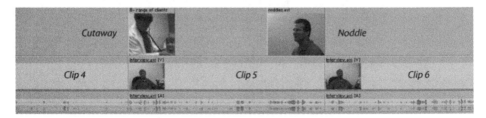

Figure 5.5. Use noddies or cutaways to hide jump cuts.

The screenshot in Figure 5.5 shows an editor that offers multiple video tracks, which makes the concept of avoiding jump cuts easier to visualize. Basically, you have three choices:

1. Insert a cutaway or noddie to obscure the first frame of the second video in the jump cut. In Figure 5.5 the cutaway video inserted at the start of Clip 5 hides the jump cut between clip 4 and Clip 5.

2. Insert a cutaway or noddie to obscure the final frame of the first video in the jump cut. In Figure 5.5, the noddie inserted at the end of Clip 5 hides the jump cut between Clip 5 and Clip 6.

3. Insert a cutaway that obscures both the final frame of the first clip in the jump cut and the first frame of the second clip (not shown).

Inserting cutaways or noddies using editors with multiple video tracks is simple. You drag the video to the target location; sever the link between the audio and the video in the inserted clip (usually a right-click command that "unlinks" the audio and video) and then delete the audio. Or, you can simply mute the audio if that is easier.

With most multitrack editors, after deleting the audio, you can click and drag the newly inserted cutaway down to the main video track to free the space and avoid inadvertently shifting the cutaway clip during subsequent edits. This is shown in **Figure 5.6**, where the cutaway and noddie are now part of the main track.

Figure 5.6. Drag the inserted clips down into the main track to free the space.

If you're working with an editor that doesn't have multiple video tracks, inserting cutaways is a bit more complicated, though most editors are up to the task. Technically, the procedure is called "insert editing," so check the program's help files or manual for that term and instructions on how to perform this edit in your tool of choice.

What if you don't have noddies or cutaways to hide the jump cut? This happens frequently when you're editing group discussions or executive brief-ings and you're trying to consolidate the footage. Typically, I'll insert a short transition, such as a dissolve, between the two clips to let the viewer know that there was a change in time, which is the basic purpose of a transition.

Briefly, transitions are effects that smooth the flow from clip to clip and can range from simple dissolves, where the first clip smoothly blends into the second, to more visual effects such as the '60s-era flower-power effects used in the Austin Powers movies. Most of the time, I'm pretty conservative with transitions and almost exclusively, stick with dissolves—especially for business videos.

Unfortunately, in jump-cut scenarios, where there's minimal change between the first and second scene, a dissolve can be practically invisible, as are most static two-dimensional effects such as wipes. In these instances, I'll either use a push transition (this pushes the first scene off the screen and pulls the second on screen), or an unobtrusive three-dimensional transition such as the cube spin shown in **Figure 5.7**.

End of first scene   Cube spin transition   Beginning of second scene

Figure 5.7. If you don't have cutaways, use a transition that makes it evident that a change in time is occurring, such as this cube spin (don't worry, the effect is more evident when you watch the video).

Producing Split Edits

A split edit is any edit where the video and audio move from one scene to the next at different times. If you watch television interviews, you'll notice that the sound and video seldom cut to the next scene simultaneously, as this is less interesting to the viewer. For example, if Larry King was asking O.J. Simpson, "Did you do it?" what you really want to see is O.J.'s face as the question is asked, not Larry King's.

Of course, Larry has the benefit of using multiple cameras so the producer can cut from camera to camera at any time. We don't have that luxury. More often than not, usually, you would ask the question in the field, get the response, then come back and record asking the question again while shooting the noddies. Showing O.J.'s face while asking the question is a classic split edit, in this case called an "L-cut" for reasons that will become obvious momentarily.

Figure 5.8 shows two clips on the timeline. O.J. declined to be interviewed for this book, so we'll have to use our doctor instead. The first clip shows me prompting, "Tell me about the quality of the small town practice." Then, both audio and video cut simultaneously to the physician as he responds, "You know, that was one of my chief concerns ..."

In **Figure 5.9**, I've extended the video from the second clip over the audio from the first, allowing the viewer to watch the doctor as I ask the question. The L-cut gets its name from the shape the audio makes in the timeline when it's extended beneath the second track. You get this whenever you cut from one scene to another on the video track, but let the audio from the first scene continue.

Figure 5.8. Audio and video cut over from one clip to another simultaneously.

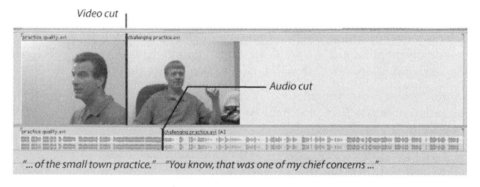

Figure 5. 9. An "L-cut" edit is where the audio from the first clip continues under the second clip, forming an L shape.

Sometimes you want the audio from the second clip to start while the video from the first clip is still showing, generally to presage the content of the second video. In **Figure 5.10**, for example the first video is Dr. Sumie commenting, "Patients really make the practice." And the second video clip is an examination where he's saying, "Breathe deeply, now."

Figure 5.10.
Creating a "J-cut," where the audio from the second video creeps under the video from the first.

Here, I've cut the audio to the second clip before the video, so while the viewer is still *watching* Dr. Sumie nod with affirmation after commenting, "Patients really make the practice," they're listening to the examination under way. The audio presages the video, which is a much more interesting presentation to the viewer. Since the audio from the second clip creeps under the first clip roughly in the shape of a J, this is called a J-cut.

When I'm editing, I use L-cuts and J-cuts as frequently as possible to avoid cutting audio and video simultaneously. Producing these split edits varies from program to program, but, as with insert edits, "unlink" the audio from both video files so that you can move the audio independently from the video.

To produce an L-cut, you adjust only the video track, as shown in **Figure 5.11**. Regardless of what editing program you use, creating an L-cut always includes these steps:

• Click and drag the right edge of the first video clip to the left a second or two to clear space for video from the second clip. Note that you're shortening the video, not dragging the entire video to the left.

• Drag the video from the second video clip over the top of the audio from the first clip.

Step 1: Drag the back edge of the first clip to the left

Step 2: Drag the front edge of the second clip to fill the space

Figure 5.11. Completing the L-cut.

With a J-cut, you adjust only the audio track, as shown in **Figure 5.12**, exactly the same way you manipulate the video to create an L-cut. Specifically:

- Click and drag the right edge of the first audio clip to the left a second or two to clear space for audio from the second clip. Note that you're shortening the first audio track, not dragging it to the left.

- Drag the audio from the second clip beneath the video from the first clip.

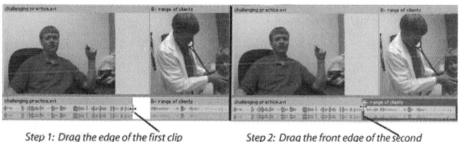

Step 1: Drag the edge of the first clip back to the left.

Step 2: Drag the front edge of the second clip to fill the space.

Figure 5.12. Completing the J-cut.

Using Transitions

As I mentioned earlier, the purpose of a transition is to clue the viewer of a change in scene or time. Unless your video includes changes in scene or time, you shouldn't insert transitions between the individual video sequences with one notable exception: to avoid a jump cut. Even then, it's better to use a cutaway or noddie rather than a transition.

The best way to understand how transitions are used in business type footage is to watch interviews on the evening news, or programs such as *60 Minutes*. You'll notice that transitions are rarely used; when they are used, they're nearly always-dissolves or fades to black.

Inserting transitions is generally very simple. Typically they sit in their own library or collection bin, and you simply drag them into the timeline or story-board between the two clips.

5. Create Titles and Credits

Titles are text screens that convey information such as the title of the video, closing credits, locations, and the names and positions held of people appearing onscreen. Virtually all video editors have built-in titling functions that are easy to use and generally well-documented. Here we'll address implementation details like choosing a font, its size and color; where to place your titles within the video screen; and how long those titles should remain onscreen.

When producing titles, you need to consider several factors; some are mechanical and some are artistic. I'll list them here in order of importance, and discuss each point in detail below.

1. Your title must be *visible* onscreen, so it must be placed within the title-safe region.

2. The colors used must be *"broadcast safe"* so they are visible on television screens. Note that if you're producing video solely for computer playback, neither of these restrictions applies.

3. Your titles must be *legible*, which means using a font you can read in the correct size and color, and on a background to provide contrast when necessary.

4. Your titles must be *appropriate*, which means placed onscreen according, which we'll go into below.

5. Your titles should be *consistent* in all major aspects.

In this section we'll discuss the six most common types of titles:

*   *Video title*—presenting the name of the video and other pertinent details.

*   *Name/title or affiliation*—identifying the person in the video.

*   *Information screen*—essentially a text message to be read by the viewer.

*   *Bullet points*—listing items that underscore the audio portion of the video.

- *Closing credits*—naming individual(s) and organization(s) that contributed to the video.

- *Copyright text*—identifying the copyright holder and the year.

This overview provides an outline for this section; now let's jump in and look at some details.

Title and Action Safe Regions

If you're producing titles for display on a television set, either via DVD or by writing to VHS or other analog formats, note that television sets don't display the outer edges of the video—an area called "overscan." If you place your titles or graphics in the overscan area, they won't be seen by your viewers.

To help avoid this, most titling utilities can display a "safe zone" comprised of one or two boxes such as those shown in **Figure 5.13**. The innermost square is called the Title Safe region, which represents the 80 percent of the screen that all televisions should display. Position your title within this title safe area and your television viewers will be able to see it; go beyond the region, and it may be cut off.

The outer square represents the Action Safe region. Video within this outer box will most likely display without being cut off by the television set, but action outside of this box will most likely be obscured as overscan. Note also that these boxes do not actually appear onscreen after you apply the title.

Figure 5.13.
Title Safe and Action Safe regions in the title.

Note also that when a computer plays a video file, it displays all pixels in the video file. Accordingly, the concepts of overscan, title safe, and action safe are not applicaple to streaming video or other video that will never appear on a television set. While you shouldn't position your titles at the very edges of the video, a few pixels in from any side should work well.

Broadcast Safe

Simply stated, computers can display more colors than a television set, particularly the brighter spectrum of colors like red, yellow, and green. For this reason, when producing your titles on a computer, you want the colors to be safe for television, in other words or "broadcast safe." Otherwise, the color may appear distorted or may pulse visibly on the TV screen.

Many prosumer programs display warnings if you select a color that isn't broadcast safe. Such a warning is shown on the left in **Figure 5.14**. If your program doesn't provide a warning, you can ensure that your colors are broadcast safe by making sure that all three Red, Green, and Blue values have at least 15 bits of color. As shown on the right in Figure 5.14, adding color bits corrected the problem with the overly red title color in the example.

As with the title safe and action safe zones, title color isn't an issue for videos displayed solely on a computer; in this case, achieving the right aesthetics and contrast are the primary factors in choosing a color for your titles.

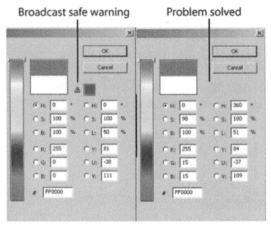

Figure 5.14.
To make your colors broadcast safe, make sure all RGB values have at least five bits of color.

Choosing a Font—Background

Your first consideration when choosing a font should be legibility, or the viewer's ability to read onscreen text. Note that this metric varies according to screen size and whether the video is compressed and to what extent. This is shown in **Figure 5.15**.

To produce Figure 5.15, I created a title using the named fonts at 36 points for the larger text, and 18 points for the smaller text. After creating the title, I rendered twice—once at 128Kbps (shown on the left), and then at 32Kbps (shown on the right), both times using Microsoft's Windows Media Format with output at 320x240 resolution.

On top is Times Roman, an "Old Style" font with serifs, the little pointy edges you can see at the ends of many of the letters. If you scanned a book or magazine, you would notice that most text is printed in Old Style fonts such as Times Roman because it is highly readable.

However, Old Style fonts have two characteristics that don't work well at high compression. First, as you can see on the right, the serifs tend to disappear at high compression, degrading the appearance of the font. In addition, if you closely analyze the font, you'll notice a variance in the thickness of some of the letters. Compare, for example, the upper left regions of lower case o's and e's with the right side of letters like lower case m's and d's. This is important, because at high compression, these thinner lines tend to disappear, degrading the appearance even further.

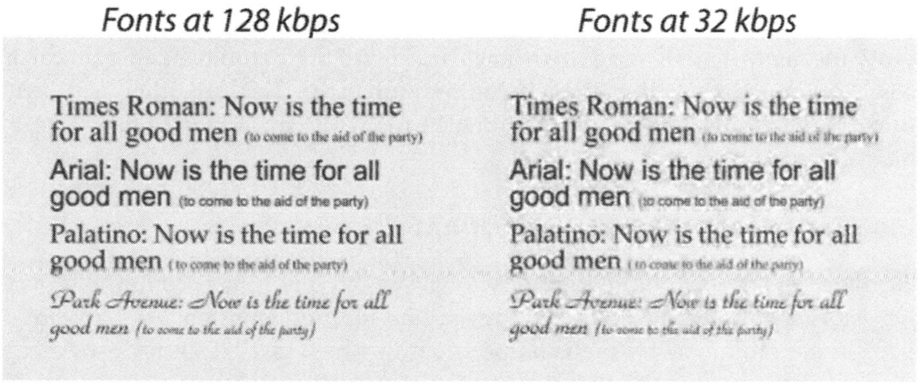

Figure 5.15. Fonts compressed to 128Kbps, on the left. and 32Kbps on the right.

Beneath Times Roman is Arial, a sans serif font. If you study books and magazines, you'll notice that most chapter and heading titles are in sans serif fonts such as Arial. That's because, as you can see in Figure 5.15, sans serif fonts stand out. In this regard, they're easier to browse than serif fonts, and better for quick hits of information, but not as readable over the long term.

For our purposes, note also that Arial, like most (but not all) sans serif fonts, is "monoweight," which means all lines are the same thickness. This makes Arial the most easily compressed font of the group, with great readability even at 32Kbps.

Next time you're watching a television program, make a mental note to determine whether they're using serif or sans serif fonts. In my experience, when the issue is readability (news, advertisements, public service announcements), sans serif fonts are used almost exclusively, as they are in most high-volume streaming media.

Back to our font comparison. I included Palatino, an Old Style font, because I like its appearance and use it frequently. It's slightly thinner than Times Roman, but otherwise shares the same characteristics regarding readability and lack of compressibility.

The final is Park Avenue, a "script" font, which means it's designed to look as if handwritten. It shares the serifs and nonuniform line size of Times Roman, but carries much more detail. Predictably, it quickly degrades at high compression ratio.

Interestingly, at 128Kbps, all fonts retain close to original quality, so with most video produced for DVD, television, or desktop viewing, post-compression readability shouldn't dictate the font. It's worth noting here that EIA-708, the FCC regulation that delineates the requirements for closed captioning on U.S. television, prescribes the use of eight font types, including serif, sans serif, and script fonts, meaning that all the fonts shown in Figure 5.15 would be "legal" for a closed-captioned feed. But at high compression rates, Arial or other sans serif fonts are the obvious choice. (See Chapter 11 for a full explanation of how to produce closed captions.)

Choosing a Font—Recommendations

Clearly there's is no absolute right or wrong way to go in font selection, but over the years I've adopted the following conventions for producing my titles. (Assume that I'm not producing for high compression (in which case I'd simply use Arial.)

- *Video title*—Since this title is usually short and large (e.g., highly readable), I use an artistic font that matches the storyline. As you'll see in the country doctor video, I used Rosewood Standard fill, a serif font with a "country" feel.

- *Name/title or affiliation*—Here I use Palatino or a similar Old Style font I made this choice solely based on aesthetics. I just like the way they look, and think Arial looks particularly dowdy in titles.

- *Information screen*—I always use Palatino, Times Roman, or another Old Style font for their overall readability.

- *Bullet points*—I go with Arial or another sans serif font for readability and common usage.

- *Credits*—Arial or another sans serif font again for the reasons above.

- *Copyright text*—Again, Arial.

Obviously, being consistent with font usage—within a single project, and among similar or related projects—is as important as your choice of fonts. For this reason, most organizations create standards regarding fonts, font sizes, colors, duration, and other title attributes.

In the next few sections, I'll show you the standards I use for most business-oriented productions. Note that many of these are my own personal preferences; as I said, there is no true right or wrong. What is important for you is to recognize the need to create and apply similar standards and consistencies in your own videos.

Many parameters like font, font size, color, and positioning need no further explanation. Before introducing my standards, let me briefly describe some parameters that may not be so obvious.

- *Template*—Most video editors have text or title templates that control title attributes like font, font size, font color, background, and positioning. If you're using a template in your production, obviously you'll want to note which one. Once you go through the process of standardizing your titles, you may also want to see if your video editor can save that information as a custom template—also a fairly common feature that will make it simple to achieve future consistency.

- *Background*—When displaying titles over video, the background behind the text is critical to title legibility. In some instances, you can use the video itself as a background, but often the colors in the video are too varied to produce the consistent contrast necessary for a legible title. For each title, I'll discuss the most appropriate background or backgrounds for the title.

- *Transition effects*—I invariably fade my titles in and out, which is simple to do in most programs. This is an aesthetic choice that you don't have to adopt, but this parameter should be considered when you select your own titling standard.

- *Animation*—Other than scrolling credits at the end of my movies, I typically don't animate my titles, so they don't fly in from the left or scroll up and down like the *Star Wars* introduction. If yours do, save the effect in the appropriate style box.

With this as prologue, let's move to the opening title sequence.

Opening Title

The opening title is used at the very start of the video (shown on the left in **Figure 5.16**). With educational or training usage, be sure to identify both the speaker and the topic, and any other relevant information to let the viewer know the subject of the video (they'll want to know what they're watching the correct video).

If your video has discrete sections you'd like separate by titles, use similar parameters, but a smaller font size, around 35 to 50 points. These are the titles shown on the right in Figure 5.16. I also use the same approach and font for the "The End" screen that I include in many productions, generally using a point size of around 50.

Figure 5.16. A video title screen on the left; section headings on the right.

Title	Opening title.
Template	N/A.
Font	Choice dictated by artistic considerations (for example, Rosewood Standard fill used in Figure 5.16 for the "country" look).
Size	40-80 points (35-50 points for section titles).
Justification	Centered.
Position	Upper half vertically, centered horizontally.
Color	Varies according to background; choose for maximum contrast.
Background	Usually displayed over video (as shown) or black background.
Duration	15-20 seconds; note that with most editors, you adjust title duration by dragging the right edge of the title to make it longer or shorter.
Insert when	At the very start of the video.
Transition effects	Half-second fade in and out.
Animation effects	None.
Miscellaneous	Use similar parameters for titles between discrete sections in the video (e.g., Introduction, Section I, Section II).

Name/Title or Affiliation

These titles identify speakers when they appear onscreen. Use a consistent background on all name titles; I prefer to make the title background semi-transparent (see the title shown on the left in **Figure 5.17**); this creates sufficient contrast to make the text readable without appearing obtrusive, though not all programs support this.

Borders around titles (such as those shown on the upper right of Figure 5.17) look good in video produced for television, but the lines degrade severely at high compression. For this reason, I also avoid drop shadows and inner and outer strokes on titles used in videos destined for high compression. Keep it simple is the best advice at high compression ratios.

Figure 5.17. This title identifies the speaker when he or she appears on screen.

Title	Name/Title or Affiliation.
Template	N/A.
Font	Palatino (Old Style) for appearance (see san-serif fonts in both titles on the right).
Size	Name-25-35 points; affiliation or title-20-25 points (go no lower than 18 points).
Justification	Left justify.
Position	Lower third, on the left; however, when multiple individuals are identified simultaneously, attempt to place the title directly beneath each individual.
Color	Choose for maximum contrast—generally white or yellow against a blue or black background for maximum legibility.
Background	Black or blue (or template), set to about 40-50% opacity.
Duration	Twice as long as it would take to read the title; 5-10 seconds max.
Insert when	A few seconds after the initial appearance (not simultaneously); if video is more than five minutes, insert again approximately every five minutes or so.
Transition effects	Half-second fade in and out.
Animation effects	None.
Miscellaneous	Always use a background to provide contrast.

Information Screen

After the opening titles comes an information screen; this is text intended for the viewers to read (**Figure 5.18**). The small caps font shown on the right is a popular technique for many information screens.

Using upper and lower case (shown on left), is considered easier to read, because readers recognize the words as words, rather than having to read the individual letters and decipher the word. Experiment with both to see which you feel is more readable.

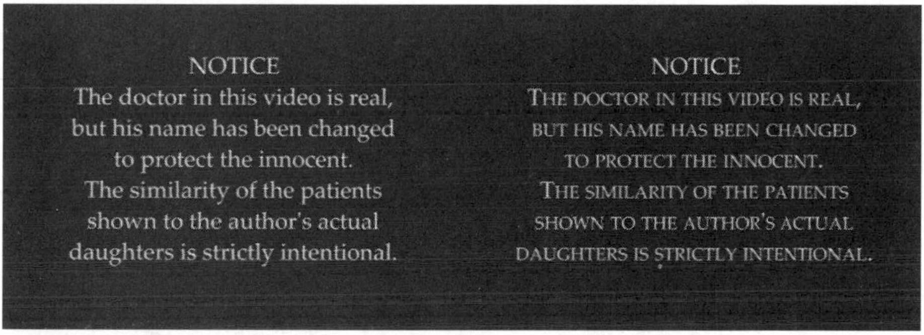

Figure 5.18. Information screen, shown in a normal font and in small caps.

Title	Information screen.
Template	N/A.
Font	Palatino (Old Style font) for readability.
Size	30-35 points; aim for no more than 30-35 words per screen.
Justification	Center.
Position	Center.
Color	White.
Background	Black.
Duration	Twice as long as it takes to read the words out loud.
Insert when	If necessary, at the start of the video.
Transition effects	Half-second fade in and out.
Animation effects	None.

Miscellaneous

You may have to adjust the "leading" controls in the titling utility to achieve the vertical spacing between the lines. For example, the leading controls for both titles in Figure 5.18 were set to 10, increasing the interline spacing considerably. Controls will vary by product, but your goal should be no more than 7 to 9 lines of text per screen (and for Web output, no more than 3 to 4).

Bullet Points

Bullet points are titles introduced to highlight certain audio portions of the video. For example, while the physician in our video was outlining the benefits of the small town practice, you might produce a title with the bullet points shown in **Figure 5.19**.

While you can certainly build these titles against a flat black or blue screen, I like to use a thematic background, when available, as shown in Figure 5.19. When the image is too bright to provide the necessary contrast (as shown on the left), darken the background image, either within the video editing application or using an image editor, to improve readability (on the right).

Figure 5.19. Bullet-point titles shown against two backgrounds. The image on the right with the background darkened , is much more legible than the one on the left.

Title	Bullet points.
Template	N/A.
Font	Arial or similar sans serif font for fast word recognition.
Size	Title should be between 45-55 points, bullet points 35-45.
Justification	Left (center is also popular, so the choice is up to you).
Position	Vertical Center, horizontal on the left.
Color	White.
Background	Solid or thematic background dark enough to provide contrast.
Duration	Keep up as long as relevant to the audio.
Insert when	To correspond with audio.
Transition effects	Half-second fade in and out.
Animation effects	None.
Miscellaneous	As with PowerPoint slides, you also need to set a capitalization policy. I generally capitalize all words in the title (except ands, ins, and similar prepositions), and only the first word of each bullet point, plus proper nouns.

Closing Credits

Closing credits generally don't contain mission-critical information, so you're free to get a bit more creative. A range of font and background options are shown in **Figure 5.20**. The options in the style guide are those used in the larger title on the left.

Figure 5.20. Closing credits are less formal than other titles, allowing greater creative leeway.

Title	Closing credits.
Template	N/A.
Font:	Sans serif font such as Arial.
Size	20-35 points.
Justification	Center.
Position	Center.
Color	White.
Background	Appropriate background from video or solid black or blue. If you have interesting footage (post-interview conversation, etc.), most programs support the split-screen approach shown on the bottom right of Figure 5.20; this give's your video a very professional look.
Duration	Twice as long as it takes to read the words. Almost invariably, you adjust duration by dragging the right edge of the title to make it longer or shorter.
Insert when	After "The End."
Transition effects	None—scroll in and out.
Animation effects	Scrolling.
Miscellaneous	Many producers scroll credits while showing video from the interview, discussion, or briefing in the background. To produce the contrast, you may need to darken the video slightly using the video editor's brightness and contrast controls.

Copyright Notice

Technically, all video is copyrighted whether or not it contains a notice like that shown in **Figure 5.21**. Nonetheless adding copyright notices "discourage" copyright infringement, or the use of your video without your written permission. It also keeps legal types off your back, and insulates you from barbs from bosses or co-workers asking, "Where's the copyright notice?"

To be complete, the copyright notice must contain the copyright "bug" © or the word copyright, plus the year of creation and the name of the copyright holder. I go beyond that with the large copyright notice shown on the left in Figure 5.21, moving towards a more minimalist approach on the upper right.

Figure 5.21. Various versions of the copyright notice; the notice on the upper right contains the minimum required information.

Title	Copyright notice.
Template	N/A.
Font	Sans serif font such as Arial.
Size	20-25 points.
Justification	Center.
Position	Center.
Color	Center.
Background	Appropriate background from video or solid black or blue.
Duration	5-10 seconds. Almost invariably, you adjust duration by dragging the right edge of the title to make it longer or shorter.
Insert when	After closing credits.
Transition effects	Fade into copyright notice; fade to black after notice.
Animation effects	None.

Customizing Titles for Streaming

When producing video and titles for streaming video, keep these points in mind.

The good news is that streaming video is almost always watched on a computer screen, which displays much greater detail than a television set. However, when producing for low-bitrate streaming at reduced resolutions, such as 320x240, you're essentially cutting the point size of your fonts in half. That's because when you shrink the video from 640x480 to 320x240, you shrink everything in the video by 50 percent. This means your highly readable 20-point font becomes a tiny, smudged-looking 10-point font.

Regular font

Bold font

Figure 5.22.
Bold fonts compress with much greater legibility than normal fonts.

This won't matter for larger titles like the opening title and bullet points, but will affect many smaller titles, particularly name/affiliation tags. When producing for a 320x240 window, boost the point sizes for these titles by about five points for improved legibility. In addition, consider bolding the text, because bold text survives compression with much greater legibility. This is shown in **Figure 5.22**, where both video files were compressed to 32Kbps.

Though it will seem like the larger font size is consuming gobs of space, remember that you can ignore the safe zone when you're working with streaming video (since it isn't displayed on a television set). For this reason, you can reclaim the space by moving the title much closer to the bottom or left edge of the video.

6. Add Logos and Still Images

Many organizations place their logo over all videos, which is typically called a watermark. Most editing programs except for Microsoft's Movie Maker 2, which doesn't offer this function allow you to do this fairly easily.

Most programs use a feature called "overlay" or "chromakey" to superimpose the still image over the background video; I explain this fully in Chapter 6. As they relate to video, chromakey and overlay can get pretty complicated. However, using these techniques with still images is simple.

To use chromakeying, produce your logos over a solid blue background. I'll show you how to achieve this in a moment. Alternatively, if you know how (or if a graphics artist is creating the logo), save the logo as a 32-bit TGA (Targa) file with a transparent background alpha channel.

Briefly, an alpha channel specifies which portion of the image should be transparent when merged with another image or video. With a logo file, you (or your graphics artist) would designate the background of the image as transparent, so when merged with the video file, all but the logo will disappear.

To insert the logo into your video project, drag it onto a separate video track above the main video track, (shown in **Figure 5.23**). As with titles, typically, you adjust duration by dragging the right edge of the logo to make it longer or shorter. If your program doesn't have multiple video tracks, check documentation for "adding logos" or "overlaying still images" onto your video.

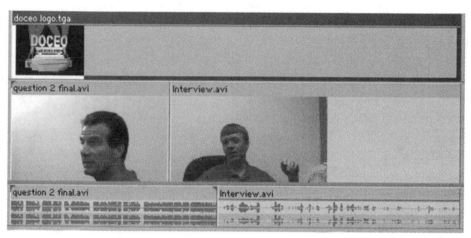

Figure 5.23. To insert your logo in a prosumer editor, drag it to a track above the video.

If you create a 32-bit image with an alpha channel, most video editors will recognize that you want the background eliminated, and do this automatically. If you create an image with a blue or black background, after placing the image on the timeline, you'll see the logo with background superimposed over the video, as you see on the left in **Figure 5.24**.

To eliminate the background, use the chromakey filter, (which I'll explain in the next chapter) program controls to apply the video editor's chromakey filter to the logo. At a high level, these tools work by eliminating a color from the top video and inserting what's not eliminated into the background video. Operationally, the first step is to identify the color you want removed from the logo, typically using an eyedropper or similar tool like that shown on the left in Figure 5.24.

With still images, the background is perfectly consistent, so selecting it with the eyedropper usually makes the background disappear immediately. If not, find the filter's "similarity" or "color tolerance" adjustment, which expands the range of colors excluded by the chromakey filter. Increase the tolerance control slightly and the background should completely go away.

Once you've eliminated the background color, use the program's two-dimensional (2D) motion controls to shrink the image to the desired size and move it to the target location, making sure that you're within the Action Safe region. To make the image translucent, find the program's transparency control and adjust it to the target value. A translucent logo is shown on the image on the right in **Figure 5.25**.

Figure 5.24. After applying the chromakey filter, use an eyedropper or similar tool to select the background color to eliminate.

Figure 5.25.
Logo, after shrinking and moving to the right bottom corner (left), and then adjusting the transparency values (on the right).

Adding Full-Screen Images to Video

Virtually all video editors can import digital images and convert them to video. This includes not only digital pictures and logos, but also the output of programs such as PowerPoint, Visio, AutoCAD, and other electronic design programs. Adding images to video is a great way to explain your work or product and can help break up otherwise monotonous talking-head footage.

Adding still images to your editor is also fairly simple. Generally, you drag them down to a video track and grab the right edge to set duration. Most programs let you add transitions between still images and adjust color, brightness, and similar values with the same filters available for video.

However, when adding line art and other finely detailed images, you must keep several critical points in mind. First, the resolution of video is limited. Even a high-quality format like MPEG-2 (used in DVD) has a resolution of 720x480 pixels, while streaming files are often produced at 320x240 pixels. Suppose you included a high-resolution image such as an architectural drawing produced in AutoCAD 2004 shown in **Figure 5.26.**

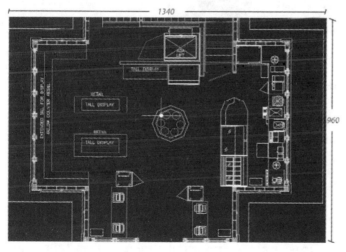

Figure 5.26.
Output from AutoCAD 2004.

The image has a resolution of 1,340x960. If you're encoding for DVD at 720x480 resolution, there aren't enough lines of pixels in the video file to display all the pixels in the image. To convert from the 1,276x820 source to the 720x480 output during encoding, the video editor will discard image detail, degrading image quality.

Plus a television set's inability to display fine details with accuracy only compounds the problem. Basically, it's almost impossible to display high-resolution images in a video file without losing detail.

To workaround, cut your image into smaller chunks as shown in **Figure 5.27**. Then, import the files into your video editor and display them in the desired order.

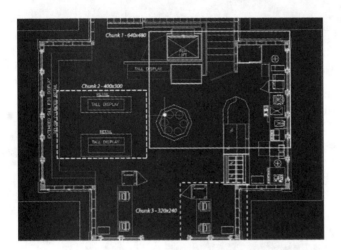

Figure 5.27.
To show a high-resolution image, display it in chunks.

You can do this in two ways. First, divide the image up into separate images—each containing the desired views—using an image editor like Ulead's PhotoImpact or Adobe Photoshop. When using this approach, keep the following rules in mind:

- For best results, make sure each image has an aspect ratio of 4:3, meaning four horizontal pixels for every 3 vertical pixels. Figure 5.27, for example, includes chunks of 320x240, 640x480, and 400x300, all of which adhere to the 4:3 ratio. The easiest way to calculate this is to divide the number of horizontal pixels in the image by four, then multiply by three to produce the desired vertical resolution.

- Also, make sure each image has a lower vertical resolution than your target output. If producing for DVD, this means less than 480 lines of resolution.

- After you input each image file into your video editor, use 2D image controls to zoom the image to full screen, making sure that you zoom proportionately, meaning equally on both the horizontal and vertical axis. Otherwise, you could distort the image.

Using 2D Controls to Scan Around the Image

As you become more familiar with your video editor, you'll find the easiest way to show portions of an image is to insert a high-resolution version into the video editor and use the editor's zoom and positioning controls to show only the desired region of the image. Take a mental break for a second, and I'll explain the procedure.

Imagine you were at Mount Rushmore with your camcorder. You stand in one spot and zoom in to shoot George Washington, where it all began. Then you zoom out to show President Washington with President Jefferson. Then you zoom back in and pan across to President Lincoln, then President Roosevelt.

Obviously, the magnificent carved mountain is there the entire time; you're just using the camera's zoom controls to zoom in and out and your own two-dimensional positioning controls (hands and arms) to move the camera around the mountain. Most video editors have controls that work the same way, allowing you to pan and zoom around high-resolution images to show only low-resolution sections.

Once you've imported the image into the editor, you can zoom into and out of the image with magnification controls, and pan around the image using positioning controls. The only segment of the image the editor will include in the rendered video appears in the viewport; the other regions of the image are still there, but out of camera.

This is illustrated in **Figure 5.28**; the black area is the viewport, and the gray regions are out of the camera's current scope. Basically, you drag that portion of the image to display into the viewport, and use zoom controls to zoom into or away from the image.

The only caveat is to keep the viewport smaller than the output resolution of the video, just as you did for each subset of the image you isolated in your image editor. The image editor will automatically set the viewport to the correct output resolution, so you don't even have to worry about choosing a 4:3 ratio. This is faster and simpler, and while the interface may vary from what's shown in Figure 5.28, virtually all editors offer these controls.

Camera viewport (dark black)

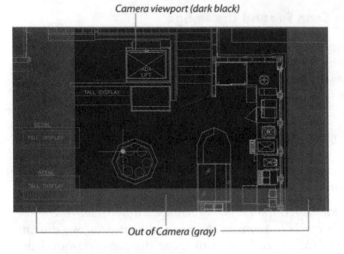

Figure 5.28.
Two-dimensional (2D) editing controls allow you to show different regions of an image at different magnification levels.

Out of Camera (gray)

7. Fading In and Out

I start almost all productions by fading in from black and end by fading to black. Some programs have a dedicated filter to accomplish this (most notably Movie Maker 2), though the predominant general technique is to apply a dissolve transition to the beginning or end of the video file. This topic should be well-documented, so if you're not sure how to fade in and out, check your manual or help file.

Once you've accomplished your first and last fades, you can skip to Chapter 7 to learn how to render your project for distribution to your viewers.

In the Workbook

The workbook for this chapter features two main components. First, there are separate pages for each titling standard discussed in the chapter, which you can use in your own productions.

Second, there are program-specific instructions for the seven editing steps as outlined in this chapter. Go to *www.doceo.com/dv101.html* for a list of currently supported video editors.

Chapter 6:
Shooting for Compositing & Streaming

Two applications require specialized shooting techniques: shooting for compositing and shooting for low bitrate streaming distribution. As you can probably guess from the title, this chapter addresses these issues.

Compositing sounds complicated, but really it's not. Simply put, it's the process of merging two videos (or a single video and still image) to display one combined video. Compositing is also called "overlay," as in laying one video over another, "chromakey" or "color key" where you use color values to discern how to combine two videos, or more specifically "green screen" or "blue screen" when using these colors in the compositing process.

This chapter starts by describing how to shoot against a green screen to produce one video you can overlay onto another. The techniques involved in actually compositing the video are highly specialized, so I'll cover the software side as well.

The final section explores different techniques for producing video that looks good even after being compressed to ultra-low bitrates for streaming, and how working with composited video may actually yield improved quality at low bitrates. I'll share the results of some extensive green-screen and black-screen testing, and provide some clear guidelines for producing the best possible streaming video quality.

Shooting for Compositing

At a high level, compositing combines two videos by eliminating portions of one video, and placing the remaining portions over the other video. For example, in **Figure 6.1**, we'll combine the video on the left over the video in the middle to create the video on the right.

You can't see it in Figure 6.1 (because the book isn't in color), but the background behind the image on the left is solid green. When compositing the two videos, I'll use a chromakey filter to remove everything that's green in the video on the left and overlay the remaining portion- just the video of me, on the video of the building in the middle.

Figure 6.1. Compositing takes one video (on the left), eliminates the chromakey color, and imposes the remaining video over a background video (middle) to produce the composition on the right.

What are the keys to good keying? There are three I'll briefly mention and then cover in detail below. The first is simple: the object being keyed can't contain any colors that are similar to the background video; otherwise, those colors will be eliminated along with the background. So if you have a bright green background and wear a bright green shirt, you'll look like the invisible man from neck to navel.

Second, the background has to be relatively consistent. If you use a cloth background, it must be flat against the wall, smooth, and wrinkle-free. If the background is painted, there should be no chips, bumps, or uneven sections.

Finally, you need a clean video signal, which means a decent camera. If you attempt to shoot green-screen video with an inexpensive DV or analog camcorder, you'll likely be disappointed with the results.

Now that we've got the high level down, let's take a closer look at the details.

The Background

Chromakey backgrounds are typically blue or green. I choose green because blue is plentiful in my wardrobe and green non-existent, but I'm not religious about it. Either color will do just fine, so long as you purchase fabric or paint backgrounds specifically designed for video compositing applications from a reputable source. Hanging up a blue cotton sheet from Wal-Mart just won't get the job done. As you'll see, you don't have to spend a lot of money—we spent $20 for one of our backgrounds—but the color must be consistent.

Your choice of fabric or paint depends on the application. Paint is better if you're shooting consistently from one location, and is cheaper from a coverage perspective, though probably less so if you have to pay someone to paint the wall. Fabric is faster and more portable, and you can take it down and store it when not in use; this is ideal, given that bright green and blue don't *feng shui* very well.

Most chromakey fabric is made of muslin, a heavy fabric that hangs very smoothly. When hanging your fabric, be careful to minimize creases and folds. If the subject will be moving, or you're shooting outdoors, secure the fabric at the top and bottom to avoid motion from the wind.

For true portability, consider purchasing a collapsible or portable background. Depending on the size of the background and where you buy it, the cost can be anywhere from around $100 to several hundred dollars. Two excellent resources to compare products and prices are *www.markertek.com* for name-brand products and prices and *http://stores.ebay.com/J-and-K-Group* for less well-known products at much lower prices.

Background Size

The conventional wisdom of chromakey lighting and positioning is that the chromakey background must be lighted separately from the foreground speaker and that the speaker should be positioned six to ten feet in front of the background. The concern here is that using one light source for both subject and background would cast shadows on the background, introducing inconsistencies that complicate the chromakeying process. Unfortunately, forcing the speaker to stand 10 feet from the background significantly increases the required size of the background.

Figure 6.2 shows the background I used for all of the chromakey tests shown in this book. I bought it at markertek.com for about $20. In most shots, I stood or sat about four feet in front of the wall, and shot with a tight frame to eliminate all but the green screen. I'm assuming that most readers won't have access to a green-screen studio and will have to create a similar ad hoc background.

If this describes you, take heart—the size of the background screen isn't anywhere near as important as lighting the screen and the subject correctly. So without further ado, let's move on to lighting.

Figure 6.2.
Doesn't matter if your chromakey studio cost $20 or $2,000; if it's done right, it looks like a million bucks!

Lighting

The critical point to remember when lighting for compositing is that there are two distinct issues, as shown in **Figure 6.3**. First, you have to light the background as evenly as possible to produce the most consistent image; for this, you use background lights, as shown in the example. In most instances, I prefer soft lighting over hard lighting because it's inherently more even.

Second, you have to light the subject without casting visible shadows on the background. Unlike background lighting, which has to be flat, you can use three-point lighting (key, fill, and back) on the subject, with the desired shadows and modeling.

However, when shooting in close quarters, it can be challenging to use the hard lights necessary for three-point lighting without some light spilling over onto the background. For this reason, you may find you prefer flat lighting with soft lights (that's why both frontal lights in Figure 6.3 are key lights). In either case—three-point or flat—effective backlighting is essential to create the crisp edges necessary for a high-quality chromakey.

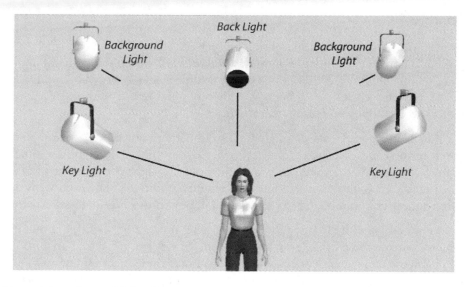

Figure 6.3. Background lights illuminate the background, while key and back lights illuminate the subject. I like flat lighting for compositing, which is why there are two key lights.

If you're attempting to insert the subject seamlessly into a specific background, consider how the background scene is lighted and attempt to match that scene's lighting in your studio with the chromakey screen. At the very least, make sure the primary lights are shining from the same direction so that the shadows all point in the same direction. For example, if the sun is streaming in from the left in the background, makes sure your key light comes from the left.

When I'm producing video for chromakey in my office, I use the fluorescent lights shown in Figure 6.2 to light the background. While the light is slightly brighter at the top of the background than at the bottom, this hasn't been a problem.

I typically sit a few inches in front of the fluorescent lights and use two soft lights at the key and fill position to produce flat lighting. I attach a clamp light with a fluorescent bulb to the shelving on the left and point is at my back as the backlight. Total cost in background and lights is easily less than $100, yet the results are as good as or better than some I've seen shot in expensive studios.

Camera

Even if your background and lighting are perfect, if the image acquired by the camera is noisy, the quality of the overlay will suffer. We used two cameras in our tests, a Sony DCR-VX2000 (a three-chip prosumer), and a very old Sony DCR-TRV9 one-chip consumer camera. We got very good results with the VX2000, while the TRV9 proved totally inadequate.

It's possible that some newer single-CCD camcorders can produce video that's good enough for a clean chromakey, especially if the scene is professionally lighted, which naturally helps to negate the poor low-light performance of most consumer camcorders. Under most real-world conditions, however, consider using a three-chip camcorder in the Canon GL2 or Sony VX2100 class or better.

Before shooting, white balance the camera, or set it to indoor lighting if manual white balance isn't available (even if you're compositing the video over an outdoor scene). We used automatic focus in our shots, but if the subject's sideways movements may cause the camera to go in and out of focus, switch to manual focus.

Use manual exposure controls as well, otherwise the camera will adjust exposure when minor motions like a tilt of the head or waving hands change the balance of light and dark regions in the frame. As we've already mentioned, the chromakey process works by "keying" out a color from the video and overlaying the portion of the video that's not that color on the background video. Chromakeying works best when the background color is as consistent as possible; this limits the range of colors the software has to exclude.

In automatic exposure mode, even visually imperceptible changes in exposure brighten or darken the green background slightly, expanding the range of colors the software has to exclude. This puts a heavy load on the software, and can degrade the results. Using manual exposure avoids this issue.

Otherwise, advise your subjects to avoid wearing clothing with colors similar to the background color. In addition, avoid white clothing, which can easily reflect the background color, and ask the subject to remove watches, bracelets, and other accessories that can also reflect the background color.

The Software Side

In many ways, the software side is a breeze after the hassles of setting up and shooting the video. To briefly recap, during the chromakey process, you combine two files, one containing the background video and another containing the video to be inserted into the background, often called the overlay video.

Compositing works differently in all programs, but generally follows this work-flow: Import the background video into the timeline. Then, load the overlay video onto a track *above* the background video and apply the chromakey filter to the overlay video.

Many programs offer a specific blue-screen or green-screen filter, which, in the-ory provides drag-and-drop compositing. I recommend against using these filters, because the preset values for green or blue never match those of your Video, and adjustment will always be necessary. Usually, you'll get better results faster using a generic chromakey or color-key filter.

Choosing the Color

Using generic controls, the first step is almost always to choose the background color, typically with an eyedropper or similar control. This is shown in **Figure 6.4**. Try to choose a spot roughly in the middle of the frame, especially when the light-ing is slightly graduated from top to bottom, as it is in Figure 6.4.

When you choose a pixel with the eyedropper, you choose *one* color value out of 16.7 million available colors. As you can see in Figure 6.4, this is enough to elim-inate some of the small specs on either side of my head, allowing faint glimpses at the background.

However, most of the background doesn't match the exact color value chosen by the eyedropper, the result of shadows, folds, creases, or other irregularities. To remove more of the color, in this case the green, (although, of course, this book is printed in black and white so you can't see it) you have to expand the range of colors, typically accomplished via a control labeled Similarity, or some variation on that theme.

Eyedropper

Figure 6.4.
Choosing the chromakey color with an eyedropper.

Basically, as you increase the similarity value, you're telling the editor to expand the search from the original color value chosen to additional colors adjacent to that value on the color chart. The effect is illustrated in **Figure 6.5**, which shows three shots with increasing similarity values. The image in the middle is almost there.

When adjusting the similarity value (and all chromakey values for that matter), use the program's zooming controls to focus in on problem areas like hair and the edges between the foreground image and the background.

Don't be shy with the similarity control; increase it dramatically until you see it eat into the subject itself, as shown in the image on the far right. Then you can back off and find a value that removes the color but doesn't erode the subject. Once you perform this exercise a time or two, it's easy to see why your subject can't wear clothing or accessories that are close to the background color.

Figure 6.5. Going, going, gone! Expanding the similarity value eliminates more and more of the background color, and—if you go too far—the foreground image.

If you can't find a similarity value that works well, try choosing a different starting color with the eyedropper. In addition, don't rely solely on any single frame to produce the final values. Instead, move from frame to frame to test your values, and use the program's zooming controls (see **Figure 6.6**) to analyze the detail. Compositing is more art than science, and is usually an iterative process.

Smoothing Controls

Even the middle image of Figure 6.5 looks pretty clean, we're not done. Your next concern is the edges, where the subject meets the background video. You'd like the edges to be as smooth as possible because "jaggies" make the overlay obvious, spoiling the illusion.

Most programs include a smoothing control (also known as feathering or softness) to smooth the edges, which achieves the effect shown in Figure 6.6. On the left is the original, unsmoothed image; on the right, the same image, post-smoothing. As you can see, these controls help the background and overlay videos blend together and appear more natural, fostering a convincing compositing illusion.

Figure 6.6. Smoothing or softness controls smooth the edges between the subject and the background image, making the overlay appear more natural.

Garbage Mattes

Sometimes the edges of the overlay video are the toughest regions to eliminate. For this reason, most programs have effects called "garbage mattes" that let you draw a free-form trapezoid around the subject, such as that shown in **Figure 6.7**, with all segments outside the drawing in the overlay clip discarded as garbage, hence the name.

Figure 6.7.
Garbage mattes are very effective when you're having problems eliminating the edges of the overlay video.

Virtually all prosumer programs have a capability such as the Garbage Matte, though it may have a different name. If you find yourself going crazy trying to eliminate the outer regions of your overlay clip, find the Garbage Matte.

One other feature worth mentioning is Spill Suppression, which is generally available only on higher-end software programs. Operationally, spill suppression identifies background coloring that isn't eliminated during the chromakey process, and converts it to gray, making it much less visible.

Spill suppression is useful when you can't increase the similarity value without eliminating portions of the subject, so visible residue of the background color remains. The feature isn't widely available in the sub-$1,000 class of editors, but if you run across it, now you know what it does.

A Caveat

Whenever you composite one video over another, there's a risk the overlay process will change the background image in some undesired way. An example of this is shown on the right edge of **Figure 6.8**, where I've moved the overlay video to the left to compare regions of the background image that are covered by the overlay video, and those that were not.

As you can see, the overlay darkened the background video slightly, which is visible in both the sky and the parking lot. Since the effect is subtle, you probably wouldn't notice it unless you actually shifted the overlay video and looked for it. For this reason, I recommend you do just that whenever you apply a chromakey effect.

Figure 6.8.
Note that the region on the extreme right of the video looks brighter than the rest. That's compositing residue.

In fact, this is my main concern with programs or plug-ins that "automatically" calculate the optimal chromakey settings for you; almost invariably, they leave some residue. It's easy enough to fix, but unless you specifically look for it, you may not notice it's there.

Shooting for Streaming Video

Compositing is traditionally used to place your subject in a different environment. One question I'm frequently asked is whether compositing techniques can also produce higher-quality video than noncomposited footage when compressed at the low bitrates required for streaming video. It's an important question, given that the type of business and educational video we're creating here is increasingly delivered via streaming media. Here's the general rule of thumb for creating low bitrate composited video.

Video with limited motion compresses more effectively than video with lots of motion. If you shoot against a green screen and superimpose that video on top of a still image, then encode the result, the entire background doesn't move, which should allow the codec to concentrate on the foreground subject and produce higher-quality video.

To test this theory, we shot two videos live, one indoors and the other outdoors. Then, we shot video against a green screen and composited that video over a bitmap image of the indoor and outdoor background used in the live shoots. We compressed all files to 100Kbps at 320x240 resolution using Microsoft's Windows Media Video codec. You can compare the results shown in **Figures 6.9** and **6.10**.

In both instances, the composited video is sharper, particularly in the outdoor setting where the wind was blowing the trees in the background, creating motion that's a challenge to compress.

Note that these qualitative differences become more important as the data rate drops. For example, at 500Kbps—a fairly high data rate for 320x240 video—the quality difference between the two videos is minimal. Note also that unless you have a live compositing device, these techniques are useless for live broadcasts. Overall, however, compositing is a great way to boost low bitrate quality.

Figure 6.9. The video on the left is live. On the right, the same clip is composited over a still image of the same background.

Figure 6.10. The video on the left is live; the video right is shot against a green screen and composited over a bitmap of the background.

The Black Screen

If you're looking for absolute quality, production efficiency, and the ability to stream video live without a real-time compositing device (and don't need to impose your subject on a different background), consider this approach to providing a clear, crisp image at much lower bandwidths: shooting against a black screen.

Specifically, I mean a nonreflective black background such as that shown on the left in **Figure 6.11.** It costs around $29 on eBay (search under "black muslin video background").

Figure 6.11. Video shot against a black screen delivers the absolute best low bitrate quality.

When shooting against a black background, use either three-point or flat lighting on the subject, but don't light the background. Don't worry if some light inadvertently spills on the background since the fabric will soak it up.

As you can see in Figure 6.11, not only is the face significantly clearer than the best image we produced via chromakey technique, the edges around the shoulders are much sharper. Also, the video was easier to produce, because there was no compositing, and the background works for live shoots.

Budget extra time the first time you shoot against a black background to get the lighting and your camera's exposure setting right; you'll find the contrast between the lighted face and black background is severe—more than most cameras can handle in automatic mode. It took me about 20 minutes to get the settings right the first time I tried.

If you can, bring a television set to attach to your camera, because relying on your LCD panel under these extreme conditions is not advised. However, as the results show, the effort is clearly worth it.

Both videos in Figure 6.11 were compressed to 100Kbps at 320x240 resolution. **Figure 6.12** shows the same video compressed down to 32Kbps (video only, no audio) at the same resolution. As you can see on the left, you still get pretty good quality even at this data rate, but only if the subject is still. Throw in even normal facial and hand motion (on the right) and image quality quickly degrades.

Overall, when shooting for low bitrate quality, think chromakey if you have to include a background image. For top-quality, live streaming, and a more efficient production workflow, however, shoot against a flat black background.

Figure 6.12. Even at 32Kbps, the video (on the left) looks good, as long as the subject doesn't move (on the right).

In the Workbook

The workbook for this chapter includes program-specific instructions for applying the chromakey effect in each video editing program. Go to *www.doceo.com/dv101.html* for a list of currently supported video editors.

Chapter 7:
Rendering Your Projects

So, your production is finished, and it's time to render your video and send it off. In years past, this was the time when your knees really started shaking, because rendering your file involved multiple obscure parameters such as GOP order and M and N values presented as life-or-death decisions in your video editor.

Recently, software developers recognized that most key compression decisions can be reduced to templates and presented in plain English. Unfortunately, just because a video editor has a template doesn't make that template right for your project. Some editors implement bad decisions, such as using nonsquare-pixel output resolutions (explained later) and some simply choose poor output parameters, such as resolutions that are too small, or data rates that are too high.

For these reasons, you must understand compression basics to guarantee producing top-quality files. To address this, I'll cover some basic concepts first, then describe how to produce video for specific uses—such as distribution via streaming or for desktop playback—and how to produce files that you can import into a DVD authoring program.

Video Compression Basics

We covered basic file parameters in Chapter 4, but now it's time to apply them, so let's review. Any time you encode a file, you'll choose a number of output parameters. **Figure 7.1** presents many of these parameters in a screenshot from Sorenson Squeeze. This is a popular encoding program used by many producers, particularly those producing multiple files in multiple distribution formats such as MPEG-2, RealVideo, Windows Media, QuickTime, and MPEG-4.

From a workflow perspective, producers using Squeeze typically output video from their video editors in DV format, and then import these files into Squeeze to produce video in the ultimate target format. If you're encoding directly from your video editor, or using a third-party encoding tool, the key parameters discussed below will be presented in a different interface, but should be easy enough to find.

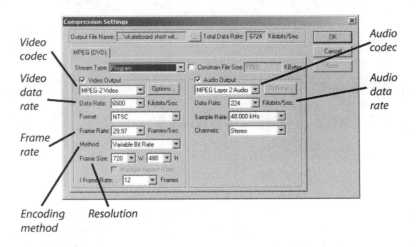

Video codec

Video data rate

Frame rate

Encoding method   Resolution

Audio codec

Audio data rate

Figure 7.1. Encoding parameters from Sorenson Squeeze 3.5, a easy to use high-quality encoding tool.

Figure 7.1 displays the most relevant encoding parameters you'll typically access when rendering files for distribution.

- *Video codec*—This is your choice of video compression technology, such as MPEG-2, MPEG-4, or Windows Media video. In Figure 7.1, I'm encoding using MPEG-2.

- *Video data rate*—This is the amount of video data associated with each second of video (also called bitrate). All video codecs are lossy and visually degrade as the data rate gets smaller, so the video data rate is a key determinant of video quality. The data rate is also critical when distributing your video over fixed-bandwidth media, such as over modems that can only send and receive data up to 56Kbps. If the data rate of your video exceeds the capacity of the distribution medium, the video will stop in mid-transmission. Note that while Squeeze lets you input audio and video data rates separately, some programs include audio and video in one overall data rate.

- *Resolution*—This is the width and height of the pixels in each video frame. Sometimes resolution is dictated by format, as with DV files, which are always 720x480. When producing streaming files, however, many producers opt for a lower resolution such as 320x240.

- *Frame rate*—This is the number of frames per second displayed in the video file. All NTSC (the standard for video in North America) DV files start with 29.97 frames per second (fps), but when producing for streaming, you'll reduce the frame rate to 15fps or lower. To achieve this rate, the editor will exclude (or drop) every other frame in the video from the rendered file during encoding, which improves the quality of the surviving frames.

- *Audio codec*—This is the compression technology applied to the audio track. Often, this decision is buried within a template, though sometimes—primarily in DVD production—you'll have the ability to choose a separate audio codec. (MPEG Layer 2 isn't necessarily your best choice for audio compression—see Chapter 8 for more on audio codecs—but Sorenson Squeeze offers limited audio encoding options.)

- *Audio data rate*—Generally, when you can choose an audio codec option, you can also choose the audio data rate.

- *Encoding method*—You have two choices for encoding, constant bitrate (CBR) and variable bitrate (VBR). You should choose VBR whenever possible.

These are the basic file parameters presented in most encoding decisions. I'll discuss these parameters and others such as keyframe setting and selecting the audio sample rate and channel in the following sections.

Advanced Encoding Parameters

As well as the basics mentioned above, you'll often see additional encoding controls that impact the quality and/or the compressed file size. Take CBR encoding compared to VBR encoding. As the names suggest, CBR applies a consistent data rate over the entire video file, while VBR adjusts the bitrate according to scene complexity. Both deliver a similar total file size, though the data rate at any given point in the file will probably be different.

Figure 7.2 illustrates the differences between the two, showing one CBR stream and one VBR stream, both produced at an average data rate of 6Mbps (megabits per second); this is the typical data rate for MPEG-2 streams prepared for DVD. As you can see, the CBR stream stays at 6Mbps throughout the entire file, while the VBR stream changes frequently. During the first talking-head sequence, which has little motion, the data rate may drop to 4Mbps or less, while increasing to 8Mbps for subsequent higher motion sequences.

VBR can steal bits from the low-motion sequences to give to the high motion sequences, delivering a more consistent quality over the duration of the video. In contrast, CBR produces a consistent bitrate, but quality varies according to scene complexity.

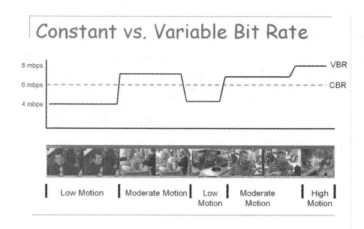

Figure 7.2.
VBR varies the bitrate according to the scene's complexity, while CBR encoding applies a consistent bitrate throughout.

What are the downsides of VBR? For this type of encoding to work well, the codec must scan through the video file twice (called two-pass encoding)—once to identify the high- and low-motion sequences and compute the optimal data rate allocation—and then to encode the video. This means that VBR encoding usually takes longer than CBR.

It's also worth noting that VBR encoding only starts to pay dividends with longer files, usually 10 minutes or longer. When encoding shorter files,—those one or two minutes long—you probably won't notice any quality difference at all.

The Many Flavors of VBR

There are several varieties of VBR and those differences require further explanation. For example, VBR works best with two-pass encoding, but many programs also provide an option for "one-pass" VBR—this encodes more quickly but produces an inferior data rate allocation between high- and low-motion sequences. Unless you're in a terrible hurry, always opt for two-pass encoding.

The three types of VBR encoding, are shown in **Figure 7.3** and explained here:

*   *Quality VBR*—Quality VBR is a one-pass VBR technique where you choose a quality metric, usually a number between 1 and 100, which the encoder then translates to a quality value that's consistently applied to the entire video. As you would expect, this means a lower data rate for low-motion sequences and a higher data rate for high-motion sequences. In Figure 7.3, you set the quality value using the slider bar currently set to 100. Quality VBR produces consistent quality, which is ideal for archival purposes, but not practical for delivering video over bandwidth-limited media such as DVD.

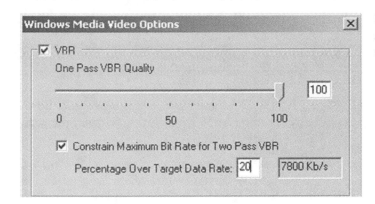

Figure 7.3.
Advanced VBR
encoding parameters

- *Bitrate VBR (Peak)*—This two-pass technique allows you to choose a target bitrate and a maximum bitrate, making it ideal for DVD delivery. In Figure 7.1, I chose 6,500Kbps for the target video data rate. In Figure 7.3, I chose a maximum data rate of 20 percent over that value, or a total video data rate of 7,800Kbps. When combined with the audio data rate of 224Kbps, this keeps the maximum total data rate to around 8,000Kbps, the maximum you should use for DVD production, because many DVD players will sputter on video encoded at higher rates.

- *Bitrate-based VBR*—If I didn't check the Constrain Maximum bitrate checkbox, Squeeze would have produced a file that averaged 6,500Kbps, but might also include regions with data rates beyond the 8,000Kbps limit. Since these data "spikes" can prevent smooth playback on certain DVD players, bitrate-based VBR is not a good choice for output to DVD.

Square-Pixel Output

Now that you know what VBR is and how and when to use it, let's tackle the optimal resolution for your video output—a surprisingly complex topic with some unexpectedly simple answers. Feel free to read ahead to the takeaways if you're familiar the explanation.

It all starts with DV, which has a pixel resolution of 720x480 and a pixel aspect ratio of 4:2.66. (To calculate the aspect ratio, divide 720 by 4 and get 180, and then divide 180 into 480 to get 2.66). However, NTSC television has a display aspect ratio of 4:3. That's why if you measure the active screen on your television set, you'll get results like 8"x6" for the 10" diagonal TV set in the kitchen, and 16"x12" for the 20" set in the bedroom. Do the math on both of these sizes, and you get 4:3 (divide 16 by 4, which equals 4, then 12 by 4, which equals 3).

So how does DV, with a frame aspect ratio of 4:2.66, display on a TV set with a 4:3 display aspect ratio? During display, the television set squeezes each line horizontally by about 11 percent. For this reason, NTSC pixels are said to be rectangular. In contrast, computer monitors display each video pixel at an even height and width, creating the so-called square pixels.

Here's the problem. Display a 720x480 DV frame on a television set, and the set squeezes the frame to look like it's about 640x480 in resolution. Display the same frame on a computer screen and it looks 720x480.

This is shown in **Figure 7.4**, which contains two pictures of my good friend Lisa. On the left is a frame extracted from the original DV file, which has a resolution of 720x480. On the right is a digital image of a television displaying the same frame. As you can see, Lisa looks noticeably more slender on the right, courtesy of the 11 percent squeeze that occurs when you display DV on a television set.

In essence, DV displayed on a television set looks "right" because it's squeezed by 11 percent before display. However, computers don't squeeze the pixels before display, so they look stretched in appearance, (shown on the left in Figure 7.4), unless you correct them.

Now you understand the background, what are the takeaways?

- First, when producing video for display on a television set, you should produce the video files at 720x480, the original resolution of DV and the resolution of MPEG-2 video used for creating DVDs.

- Second, when producing for display on a computer screen, you should always squeeze the video into an aspect ratio of 4:3, whether 640x480, 480x320, 320x240, or 176x132. You don't crop out a 4:3 region; you simply render each frame at the 4:3 ratio; this essentially duplicates the same 11 percent squeeze that televisions perform when displaying the same frame.

Figure 7.4. The original DV frame shown on the computer screen left; the same shot squeezed by a television on the right.

It's really a no-brainer as most templates default to 4:3 aspect ratios. However, some templates still default to a nonsquare resolution such as 176x144 or 352x240, and need to be corrected. In addition, when producing MPEG-2 video for computer display, say for using in a PowerPoint presentation, you need to use 648x480 rather than 720x480 to improve the look of the video inside the presentation.

For more on this subject, go to

www.extremetech.com/article2/0,3973,10083,00.asp.

Progressive Display and Deinterlacing

Most DV footage is captured in interlaced mode, which means that the camera shoots and displays 60 fields per second. The first field in the frame contains all the odd lines in the video frame (1,3,5), spread over the entire vertical height of the television set, while the second field contains all the even lines (2,4,6). This technique produces 60 visual impressions per second, promoting the appearance of smoothness.

In contrast, computer monitors display in "progressive" mode, which means that each line displays in order (1,2,3) each time the entire screen refreshes, usually between 60 to 85 times a second. You can display interlaced video on a computer screen, but the slicing artifacts evident on the left in **Figure 7.5** typically mar the output.

Figure 7.5. The footage on the left is in interlaced mode, while the image on the right is in progressive mode after applying a deinterlacing filter. (Video courtesy of Travis White, Ulead Systems, Inc.)

These artifacts are caused by the computer's attempt to display a complete frame comprised of two fields shot 1/60th of a second apart. In high-action footage such as this skateboard video, there's a lot of movement in a short period, producing two very dissimilar images, as you can see the frame on the left in Figure 7.5.

Surprisingly, the video on the right was produced by the same video editor at the same data rate as the video on the left. The only difference is I rendered the video file on the right in progressive mode, which combined the two fields into one frame, and applied a deinterlacing filter.

Interestingly, doing one without the other isn't enough. Simply choosing progressive output wouldn't eliminate the deinterlacing artifacts shown on the left, and deinterlacing without combining the two fields would have no effect.

In short, when rendering video from interlaced sources like DV for display on a computer, always do the following:

- Render the file using progressive, rather than interlaced output.

- Apply a deinterlacing filter, if available. Some programs offer different processing options such as "blend fields," "interpolate fields," or "adaptive-fields." In these instances, check the program's help files to determine the most is appropriate method for your footage.

Interlacing artifacts are most prominent in high-motion footage, where the difference between the two fields shot 1/60th of a second apart is most pronounced. That's why I used a skateboard video to illustrate the point. If you're shooting an interview or group discussion, with low-motion footage, these issues are less relevant.

Finally, understand that not all programs allow you to output progressive video or feature deinterlacing filters. For this reason, if higher-motion sequences display the type of artifacts shown in Figure 7.4, you may have to purchase another editor or third-party tool to produce top-quality video.

Keyframes

One term you'll encounter frequently during encoding is "key frame interval." All streaming media encoders use both interframe compression, which eliminates redundancy between frames, and intraframe compression, which compresses data within a frame. For example, JPEG is an intraframe technique, and is used by several streaming codecs to supply the intraframe component of their technologies.

All *interframe* compression techniques use at least two kinds of frames, key frames and delta frames. Key frames (usually elided as one word, "keyframes") are compressed entirely with intraframe compression and don't reference any other frame in the video. In contrast, Delta frames store only the information that changed between itself and the immediately preceding frame, discarding information that's similar in the two frames.

For example, in a newsroom setting, a keyframe stores the entire image, including the background wall, the set, and all details of the newscaster. In contrast, a delta frame contains only the information that changed from the immediately preceding frame. Since the background and large parts of the speaker's head and body don't change between frames, delta frames can be very small in these low-motion sequences, which is why talking-head sequences compress so effectively.

During playback, the player first displays a keyframe to get the complete picture, and then displays the updated information from the successive delta frames. When viewers use the slider bar or other controls to move randomly through the video file, video playback must start on a keyframe, since delta frames don't contain the necessary information to display the entire frame.

We like keyframes because they add quality to the video file and make it easier for viewers to randomly play the file. We don't like keyframes because they're substantially larger than delta frames, and the more keyframe there are, the harder it is for the encoder to reach the target data rate.

In most high bitrate compression, such as MPEG-2, you typically have one keyframe (note, a keyframe is called an I-frame in MPEG-speak, as you can see on the bottom left of Figure 7.1 where the control to I Frame Rate.) In contrast, most streaming encoders insert a keyframe once every eight to ten seconds, with intervals of 40 seconds or longer fairly common. In general, I almost always accept the default values for keyframe intervals, or if a default value isn't supplied, insert a keyframe every eight seconds.

Choosing Audio Encoding Parameters

Once you move past encoding templates and start setting parameters manually, you'll find yourself frequently challenged with a confusing array of audio compression options—not only bitrate, but foreign concepts such as sampling rate and bit depth. When choosing these parameters, it's important to know what comprises an audio file.

Most audio starts out as analog, meaning the spoken word or music. When an analog signal is converted to digital, whether by using your DV camera or your computer's sound card, the signal has three characteristics, each of which affects the ultimate size of the digital audio file.

The first characteristic is sampling frequency, or the number of times per second an incoming signal is "sampled." When an audio file has a sampling frequency of 44.1kHz, it means that each second of audio is split into 44,100 chunks during digitization. As you might expect, the higher the sampling frequency, the more accurate the recording, but each chunk must be stored separately, which increases the size of the digital file. Files recorded at 44.1kHz (the standard for CD-Audio) are twice as large as files recorded at 22kHz (considered FM-quality) and four times larger than files sampled at 11kHz (AM-quality). According to Nyquist's theorem—the governing principle of digital audio sampling—for an analog audio clip to be reconstructed accurately as a digital waveform, the sampling rate must be at least twice the highest audio frequency in the clip. The good news is, your video editor will almost always spare you such calculations simply by limiting your options to the 11 to 44.1kHz (or higher) range for your sampling rate.

The next characteristic is bit depth, which describes the amount of data allocated to each sample, generally either 8 bits or 16 bits. Obviously, a 16-bit recording will be twice as large as an 8-bit recording. However, when analog audio is recorded at 8 bits, there are only 256 possible values available to store the signal $256=2^8$. In contrast, at 16 bits, there are 65,216 possible values (2^{16}).

To put this in context, imagine you were recording an orchestra complete with strings, woodwinds, brass, and percussion, with many instruments capable of an incredible range of subtle tones. If you record that orchestra at 8 bits, all samples, from alto flute to xylophone, must be slotted into one of 256 possible values. Not much room for subtlety there. At 16 bits, the number expands to 65,216, which is much more reasonable. As you would expect, CD-Audio discs use 16 bits; with a sampling rate of 44.1kHz, that means 705,600 bits for each second of sound—ample breathing room.

The last characteristic is the number of channels—stereo for left and right channels, or monaural, for one signal containing all sound. Assuming sampling frequency and bit depth are the same for both channels, a stereo signal is twice as large as a monaural (or mono) signal.

CD-quality digital audio is 44.1kHhz, 16-bit stereo, and has a data rate of 176 Kilobytes per second (1,408 kilobits per second). It's far smaller than the uncompressed data rate of video, but CD-quality audio is still huge, especially when you compare it to the bandwidths used to deliver video to certain target viewers.

For a visual explanation of these digital audio concepts, go to: *www.animemusicvideos.org/guides/avtech/audio1.html*

Subsampling for Quality

Let's put this background to work. Note that many encoding schemes let you change these parameters during encoding. For example, **Figure 7.6** shows QuickTime Pro's audio encoding screen, with the QDesign Music 2 codec selected. To set the audio bitrate, click Options on the screen on the left, which opens the screen on the right, showing a data rate of 24 Kilobits per second (Kbps).

Figure 7.6. Whenever possible, adjust sampling rate, bitrate, and number of channels before choosing a data rate (on the right).

In addition to setting the bitrate, I can also adjust the sampling rate and choose between mono and stereo. In essence, if I reduce the sampling rate from 44.1kHz to 11kHz, I reduce the number of audio samples by a factor of four. Therefore, QDesign should be able to allocate four times as much compressed data to each sample.

If you're encoding high-quality music, you may find it worthwhile to experiment with different sampling rates and numbers of channels to see if overall quality improves. At a high level, this is almost identical to your decision to reduce the video resolution from 720x480 and frame rate from 30 to 15. In both cases, you're decreasing the amount of information that the compressed data rate must describe, which should boost overall quality.

Remember, though, converting from 16-bit to 8-bit audio is generally a bad idea when it comes to music, as the trained ear can pick up the vastly reduced subtlety of the sound. For this reason, many programs, like QuickTime Pro with the QDesign plug-in, simply won't permit you to change these parameters.

As we'll see below, most compression technologies have different codecs are optimized for voice and music. Obviously, you should choose the codec best suited to your source material.

Allocating Between Audio and Video

At low bitrates, audio quality is generally more important than video quality, since most viewers expect poor-quality video at these delivery rates. So at low bitrates such as 32Kbps (to stream to a 56Kbps modem), allocating as much as 8Kbps to audio, which is 25 percent of total bandwidth, is a good decision.

As data rates increase, the allocation is largely content-driven. With most audio codecs, the quality of compressed speech doesn't really improve when you boost the data rate beyond 32 to 64Kbps. So even if I were producing a 1Mbps Windows Media stream, I would probably limit my audio data rate to 32Kbps, or around 3 percent of the total.

However, music is more difficult to compress than speech because the range of sounds is greater; when music is a significant component of the video, as in a concert, music quality becomes paramount. For both these reasons, when encoding a music video at 1Mbps, I might allocate 192Kbps of bandwidth to audio, perhaps even more.

In this regard, the optimal data rate allocation between audio and video will always be project- and content-specific. Now that you know the parameters and tradeoffs involved, I'm sure that the best allocation for your project will quickly become apparent.

With this as background, let's visit our various output options.

Output to DV Tape

After you've completed your project, you should output to DV tape to create an archival copy of the finished video or to dub your video to other formats such as VHS or Hi8. Outputting to tape requires the same hardware setup as video capture: connect your camcorder to your computer and turn it to VCR mode. From there, locate the appropriate menu command ("Output to Tape" or "Print to Tape") and follow the onscreen directions. A typical example is shown in **Figure 7.7**, a screen from Microsoft's Movie Maker 2.

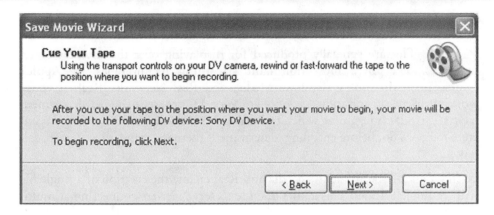

Figure 7.7. Typically, writing to DV tape is simple; here's the one-step Wizard from Movie Maker 2.

Under the hood, programs handle the write-to-tape function in different ways. Some programs use the files you originally captured or imported into the program as the starting point, and render separate "temporary" files for each effect added to your production. For example, if you added a transition between two clips on the timeline, the editor would render that transition into a temporary DV file on your hard disk.

After rendering all necessary temporary files, the program will output the entire production to the camera, reading from both the original captured files and the newly created temporary files. Other programs render a completely new DV file containing the entire project from start to finish.

Either way, producing these files can be time-consuming, easily an hour or more for every hour of video in your project. After rendering, the editor starts writing to tape in real time, so an hour of video would take an hour to write.

Writing to tape is a demanding process; if the video editor can't retrieve the necessary data from your hard disk, it will stop and display an error message. For this reason, don't store your temporary files on a network drive, and don't use your computer for other tasks while writing to tape.

Once you've finished writing to tape, you can delete all the temporary files to restore disk space, but you'll likely have to find and delete the files manually, since few programs have a function that does this on command. When you write to tape, you overwrite any previous content on the DV tape, so check the tape's contents before starting the process.

Producing Streaming Files

Streaming files are generally produced for displaying over the Internet or on intranets. The three most dominant streaming technologies are Apple's QuickTime, Microsoft's Windows Media, and Real Networks' Real. If you're working in an organization, chances are your IT experts or video department have set standards regarding which technology to use and which encoding parameters to apply. So, before encoding, determine if there is a standard and, if so, follow it.

Unlike QuickTime, Windows Media and Real enable the creation of a single file with multiple bitrates. This allows one file to serve viewers connecting at multiple connection speeds.

For example, the file about to be produced in **Figure 7.8** would contain a 148Kbps stream for viewers who connect via broadband, a 43Kbps stream the (solitary!) viewers connecting via 56Kbps modems, and a 28Kbps stream for viewers connecting at 28.8Kbps (heaven help him). This is convenient for webmasters, as it allows them to post one file instead of three. However, for this book, I'll assume most readers are interested in producing single-bitrate files, and I'll focus most of my attention there.

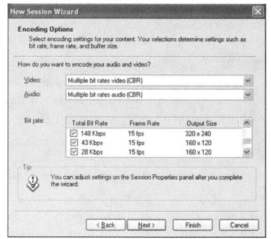

Figure 7.8.
Microsoft's Windows Media Encoder encoding a video clip at multiple bitrates in a single file.

Whatever streaming technology you select, there are some general resolution and frame-rate guidelines you should follow, which I present in **Table 7.1**. (These are suggested values, not absolute requirements.) If your encoding tool provides templates that are similar but not identical, your results should still be acceptable.

Table 7.1. Suggested resolution and frame rate for target data rates.

Target Data Rate	Video Resolution	Frame Rate
≤56Kbps	160x120	≤15fps
64-100Kbps	176x132	≤15fps
100-500Kbps	320x240	15-30fps
500Kbps-2Mbps	640x480	30fps

Also, understand that not all encoding tools provide access to all these parameters. Even when they do, file output doesn't always match the input parameters, particularly the compressed frame rate. Specifically, if you encode a high-motion file at 56Kbps or lower, most streaming codecs will reduce the frame rate dramatically to preserve individual frame quality; it's not unusual to see video compressed at very low data rates displaying only a frame or two per second.

In general, when it comes to encoding at lower bitrates, my take is that the codec developers know best. When presets are available I use them, and if the frame rate drops below the rate I've input, so be it. In some instances there may be workarounds to force a specific frame rate, but generally you're better off just going with the presets.

With these basics covered, let's start encoding files in the specific formats.

Apple QuickTime

In terms of codec selection, Apple's QuickTime is going through a changing of the guard. Historically, the most popular QuickTime video codec has been Sorenson Video 3, which is still the dominant format used by movie studios for producing trailers (**Figure 7.9**).

However, despite Sorenson Video's popularity in these circles, Apple has recently cast its lot with MPEG-4, a standard that has yet to deliver video quality near Sorenson Video 3, or RealVideo or Windows Media Video for that matter. As a result, if you're producing video in iMovie, you can't easily produce Sorenson Video 3 files, and you have to work pretty hard to produce Sorenson Video 3 output in Final Cut Pro or Compressor, Final Cut Pro's batch encoding tool. Your choices are to use QuickTime Player, a general-purpose tool that may be confusing to beginners, or a third-party encoding tool such as Sorenson Squeeze.

Let's work through the encoding screens in QuickTime Player. To encode a file, load the video file into QuickTime Player and choose File > Export from the main menu. Then click Options to open the Movie Settings screen shown on the left in **Figure 7.10**. Click Size to adjust the resolution of the output file, and Sound Settings to adjust audio parameters (see Figure 7.6).

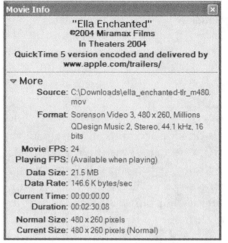

Figure 7.9.
Sorenson Video 3 and QDesign Music 2 are Hollywood's choice for QuickTime encoding.

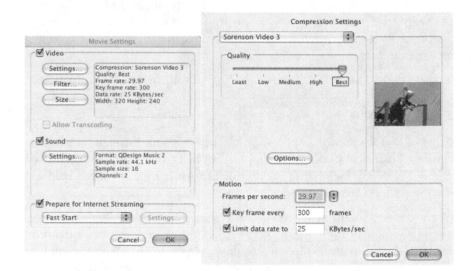

Figure 7.10. Encoding screens from the QuickTime Player.

The bottom parameter in the Movie Settings screen is the checkbox for preparing the file for Internet streaming. Use Fast Start when creating a file that will be delivered *without* a QuickTime streaming server, which will allow the viewer to start watching the file before it's completely downloaded. In contrast, when producing a file for streaming *from* a QuickTime Streaming Server, use Hinted Streaming so the server can most effectively stream the file.

With these decisions made, let's choose and configure our video codec. Click the Settings button on the top left of the Movie Settings window to open the Compression Settings screen, shown on the right. Most parameters should be familiar, save for the Quality slider. Briefly, most quality sliders either do nothing, since quality is controlled via the data rate setting, or try to improve quality by using more complex encoding algorithms that take longer to encode. Typically, documentation is sparse and you can't tell whether the quality slider actually improves quality or not, so my practice is always to set quality to the maximum setting.

I've set keyframes at one every ten seconds, and am limiting the data rate to 25KBps, which translates to 200KBps. QuickTime Player is one of the few encoding tools that uses kilobytes per second rather than kilobits, so remember to adjust your encoding parameters accordingly.

Click OK twice to close the two windows, then type the name of the encoded file, and hit Save to complete the process.

Windows Media

Microsoft's Windows Media technology provides very high-performance audio and video codecs, and as you'd expect, it's easily integrated with Microsoft applications such as PowerPoint and FrontPage. For this reason, Windows Media is generally my "go to" codec option for everything from streaming to high-bitrate files for desktop playback. Note, however, that Windows Media doesn't play on many UNIX operating systems, so if your target viewers include Linux desktop users, use RealVideo or MPEG-1 or 2.

Microsoft has done a nice job of making Windows Media technology accessible to both consumers and technology professionals. Most consumer tools provide data rate-driven templates such as those shown in **Figure 7.11**. After choosing a template, always check to make sure that the resolution is 4:3, since some templates output at 720x480 rather than 640x480, and some at 176x144 rather than 176x132. Usually, you'll see some type of information screen that provides these options, such as the Settings box shown on the bottom left of Figure 7.11.

Bytes		Bits
KB/s		kb/s
or		
KBps		Kbps
1 Byte	=	8 Bits

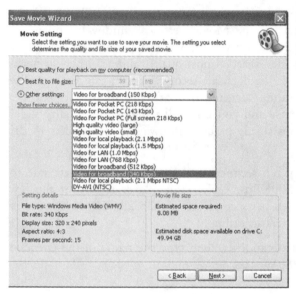

Figure 7.11.
Encoding to Windows Media format in Movie Maker 2. Note the option to produce a DV-AVI file.

Movie Maker 2 has no custom encoding parameters, so if you can't find a template you like, you're out of luck. As you can see from **Figure 7.12**, higher-end programs such as Sorenson Squeeze provide an extensive range of Windows Media format encoding options, which includes all three types of VBR encoding we discussed earlier. Here, you're free to customize encoding parameters to your liking, following the guidelines set in Table 7.1.

You can download Microsoft's Windows Media Encoder, for free at:

www.microsoft.com/windows/windowsmedia/download/default.asp.

As you would expect, the tool provides complete access to all Windows Media encoding parameters, but it's definitely targeted towards experts and may confuse novices. If you can't access the necessary encoding parameters in your consumer video editor, I recommend that you step up to either a prosumer editor or a third-party encoder such as Sorenson Squeeze.

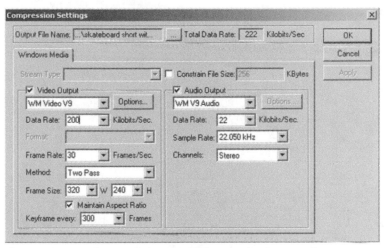

Figure 7.12. Encoding to Windows Media format using Sorenson Squeeze.

Real

Real Networks' Real technology offers arguably the best video quality at modem streaming rates, and comparable quality to Windows Media at all higher rates. This makes it very popular among large corporations and networks such as CNN and CBS. However, Real files don't integrate with PowerPoint or FrontPage (both Microsoft products) as well as Windows Media video files, so I tend to use it less for day-to-day, knock-around use.

Producing Real files is relatively straightforward, with a few twists we haven't seen before. First, when encoding within RealProducer, the company's own encoding tool (which I recommend), all rendering is template-based. Templates are called "audiences," and for each audience you can configure not only the audio/video data rate, but also alternate audio codecs and data rates to use when the audio is primarily voice or music. This is shown in **Figure 7.13**.

After you select an audience, you choose either Voice or Music mode, and RealProducer applies the selected codec and bitrate. You can also see in the figure that Real offers VBR encoding with the ability to set a maximum bitrate, which Real implements in two passes. Though not shown, RealProducer also offers a Video mode option that lets you choose between a high frame rate, with each individual frame possibly degraded (Smoothest Motion option), or a low frame rate with crisp images (Sharpest Image option). You can even produce a slideshow that will display one or two very crisp frames per second.

133

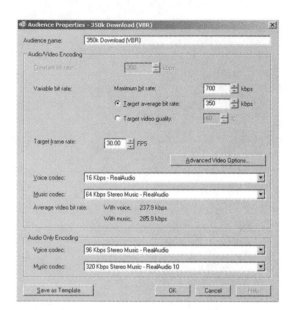

Figure 7.13. Encoding using Real Producer.

Producing MPEG-2 Files

MPEG-2 is the video codec used in DVD discs, and until recently, it was my codec of choice for desktop playback. After comparing the quality of MPEG-2 to other technologies, however, I've abandoned MPEG-2 for most desktop use, and use Windows Media instead. I recommend that you do the same (test results are here: *www.emedialive.com/Articles/ReadArticle.aspx?ArticleID=8422*). This leaves producing for DVD playback as MPEG-2's primary use.

However, when outputting a video file from an editor for input into a DVD authoring program, you should consider outputting DV files rather than MPEG-2 for several reasons. First, producing an MPEG-2 file generally takes a lot longer than producing DV. If you decide to change your video file for some reason during authoring, you'll have to re-encode the file, and waste extra time encoding.

More important, once you produce an MPEG-2 file you're locked into that data rate. Suppose, for example, that you produce your MPEG-2 files at 8Mbps, anticipating only about 60 minutes of video on your DVD. Then you decide to add some additional content, which doesn't fit because you've already encoded your video files too high. Now you're forced to either re-encode the MPEG-2 files you produced, which means double compression and quality loss, or go back to your editor and render again at a lower bitrate.

Thankfully, all this is avoided when you delay all encoding until just before producing the DVD it saves time and provides maximum design flexibility. For this reason, when working with separate editing and authoring programs, I typically output in DV format, not MPEG-2. The only caveat is that DV files are generally at least three times larger than MPEG-2, so you'll need lots of extra disk space. We'll cover producing DV files in the next section.

When producing an MPEG-2 file for DVD authoring, keep the following points in mind:

- Before encoding, check the help file of your authoring program to determine the required specifications for MPEG-2 files input into the program. For example, on the upper left of **Figure 7.14**, you see the option for Stream Type, which can either be Program (combined audio/video) or elementary (separate files for audio and video). Some authoring programs accept both, some one or the other, so check the specs beforehand to make sure you get it right.

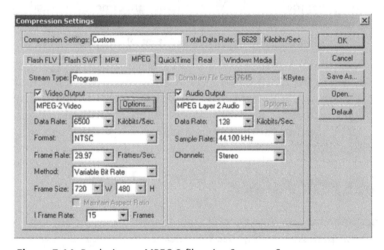

Figure 7.14. Producing an MPEG-2 file using Sorenson Squeeze.

- Use a DVD preset when available, and use default parameters whenever you can (in Figure 7.14, for example, leave the I-Frame Rate alone). The DVD specification for video is very precise, and if you adjust a parameter the wrong way, the authoring program won't accept the file.

- Always output at 720x480 resolution, in interlaced (rather than progressive) mode. Don't apply a deinterlacing filter.

- Always use VBR with a maximum data rate of no more than 8Mbps.

- Unless file size is an issue, don't use any audio compression, and output in PCM (Pulse Code Modulation) mode, the uncompressed format used for CD-Audio. If space is an issue, use the Dolby AC-3 audio codec rather than the MPEG-2 codec if both are available. I'll discuss the space available on DVD and bit-budgeting in Chapter 8.

When producing MPEG-2 files solely for computer playback, remember to output at 640x480 in progressive mode and to deinterlace the video when the option is available.

Producing MPEG-1 Files

From about 1997 to 2002, MPEG-1 was probably the most popular video codec in the universe. Today, however, it's surpassed in quality by many different technologies, including MPEG-2, Windows Media, RealVideo, and Sorenson Video 3. Its sole advantage today is that MPEG-1 files are almost universally playable, on Macs, Windows PCs, Linux desktops, and pretty much any other UNIX flavor. So, if your audience includes a broad range of playback systems, consider MPEG-1.

When rendering to MPEG-1 format, the interface should look much like Figure 7.14. Use a video resolution of 320x240, not 352x240, which is a nonsquare pixel resolution incorrectly used by many encoders. You should be able to produce very good quality at a combined audio/video data rate of 1,600 to 2,000Kbps—slightly higher if your video has very high-motion sequences.

Output to DV Format

DV format is the highest-quality, most compatible format on both the Windows and Macintosh platforms. I produce DV files for a number of purposes, including the following:

- when rendering a video file to input into a separate DVD authoring program.

- when producing a video file to input into a separate encoding program.

- when producing a video file to input into another video editor for additional processing.

In most Windows programs, you produce a DV file by first selecting the AVI format and then choosing the DV encoder. DV files are very tightly controlled to maintain compatibility between computers and camcorders, and the only encoding option you typically can configure is the audio sample rate, which can be either 32kHz or 48kHz. I always set my camcorder to capture 48kHz audio and produce my DV files at that sampling rate.

On the Mac front, both iMovie and Final Cut (Pro and Express) have presets for outputting to DV format. These make it simple to produce DV files for any of the three purposes identified above.

In The Workbook

The workbook for this chapter includes a description of each program's encoding capabilities and screenshots and information detailing the most common compression tasks.

Go to *www.doceo.com/dv101.html* for a list of currently supported video editors.

Chapter 8:
Producing DVDs

At a high level, DVDs have two components: content and menus. Content primarily takes the form of videos, slideshows, and audio files; while menus are the pages that allow the viewer to navigate to and play the content. From the same 50,000-foot view, DVD authoring comes down to two simple activities: creating the menus and linking the menus to the content so the desired video for example, plays when the viewer presses the button. Once you've linked your video content to a menu, the DVD authoring program does the rest—encoding the video into MPEG-2 format and recording menus and content to your DVD recorder.

Many consumer-oriented DVD authoring programs are just that simple—even a first-timer can create a DVD in about 10 minutes (this doesn't include the time it takes for rendering and burning, and treating the capture and editing as separate processes, even though some DVD authoring tools include those functions). As you add features to your menus, and start to customize the viewer's navigation through the disc, the creation and testing cycle gains complexity, and takes more time.

In this chapter, I discuss DVD basics like disc capacity and audio/video formats, and explore some of the advanced design and navigation options available in the more advanced authoring tools. I've structured the chapter as a large FAQ covering the most common questions I've been asked about DVD authoring and DVD-Recordable technology.

I've chosen screens from multiple programs. To best illustrate the concepts under discussion. While the concepts are consistent from program to program, the interfaces will certainly be different, and the terminology may vary slightly. My hope is that once you understand the concept, you'll know how to apply it within your authoring program of choice. For guidance specific to your authoring program, check the list of available workbooks at *www.doceo.com/dv101.html*.

About DVD-Recordable Technology

I'm going to assume that most readers will be producing DVDs to record on DVD recorders, rather than for mastering at a DVD replication facility. If you're preparing a title for mastering and replication, I recommend reading *DVD Authoring and Production*, by Ralph LaBarge (CMP Books, 2001). If you're burning your own discs, read on.

How Much Video Can I Fit on My DVD?

As much as you want to, within a few basic parameters. MPEG-2 is a scalable technology, which means you can compress to any desired bitrate. For example, to fit one hour of video on a DVD, you might encode at 8 Megabits per second (Mbps); to fit 2 hours, at 4Mbps; or to fit 4 hours, at 2Mbps.

Of course, the video starts to look pretty awful below 4 to 5Mbps unless you have stellar source material and a top-of-the-line hardware VBR encoder (typically, only Hollywood movies can go this low and get away with it). Some encoders simply won't compress below a certain rate. There are other factors mitigating the number of minutes of video you can place on disc. If you want a quick look at the bitrate you'll need to fit between 60 and 120 minutes of video on a disc, flip to **Table 8.2**.

What's the Storage Capacity of DVD-Recordable Discs?

That depends upon the type of recorder you have, as shown in **Table 8.1**. However, let's start with the mastered discs, so you'll understand the advantage Hollywood enjoyed over most smaller producers until very recently. (There are five kinds of mastered discs; the three not mentioned here, DVD-10, DVD-14, and DVD-18, are rarely used and we're not going to concern ourselves with them here.)

Table 8.1. Capacity of mastered and recordable discs.

	Mastered Discs		Recordable Discs	
Disc type	DVD-5	DVD-9	DVD±R/RW	Dual-Layer
Number of layers	1	2	1	2
Capacity	4.7GB	8.5GB	4.7GB	8.5GB
Video at 8Mbps (in minutes)	74	135	74	135

Mastered discs are mass-produced in a DVD replication facility, and most Hollywood DVDs that contain any kind of "extras" beyond the movie itself use the dual-layer DVD-9. Dual-layer discs contain data on two separate physical layers on a single side of the disc for a total disc capacity of 8.5GB. During playback, all set-top and computer DVD players first read the top data layer from the center of the disc outward. After reading all the content in the top layer, the player automatically refocuses and starts reading the bottom layer from the outside of the disc inward. This is called opposite track DVD, because the laser reads the two layers in opposite directions. The first layer has to contain at least as much content as the second layer so the laser can refocus without repositioning itself to make a seamless transition to the video on the second layer. You may notice a slight hiccup in the video when the player switches layers (although the latest players handle the layer break better than older players). Hollywood producers typically attempt to hide the break by placing it during a fade to black.

Some discs are designed to be read in the same direction on both layers, usually because the primary content of the disc is not a linear movie, but shorter video clips randomly accessed by the user. This is called parallel track; it's much less common, and *always* makes a player hiccup if read sequentially, because the laser has to refocus *and* reposition itself.

Industry Improvements

Until mid-2004, the maximum capacity of DVD-Recordable discs was 4.7GB, roughly 55 percent of the capacity of a mastered DVD-9. This huge difference started to become relevant to projects involving around 2 hours of video, because you had to drop the bitrate (and, thus, the quality) to squeeze the video onto the disc. For example, with 8.5GB of capacity, you can encode two hours of video at about 8.5Mbps, which should deliver absolutely flawless video quality. To fit 2 hours of video on 4.7GB, however, you'd have to encode at 4.7Mbps, a much lower rate that would visibly degrade the video.

In 2004, however, several vendors started to ship new DVD-Recordable drives that supported recording to dual-layer (DVD+R DL) discs with a storage capacity of 8.5GB, the same as a mastered DVD-9. Early adopters were punished with the usual incompatibility problems that plague most new formats, but the second-generation drives and discs improved matters considerably. Reviewing a first-generation drive, *EMedia* magazine reported about a 35 percent success rate in terms of playback of recorded dual-layer discs with consumer DVD players in June 2004. By September, second-generation drives were returning about a 65 percent success rate, which looks better, but still means you should proceed with caution. What's more, the price difference between single and dual-layer media remained quite large, with dual-layer media costing more than $15 per disc compared to less than $1 for recordable media in high quantities.

Surprisingly, the price difference between single-layer and dual-layer *recorders* isn't that significant. Since all dual-layer recorders can also record to single-layer recordable and rewritable discs, buying a dual-layer recorder is a no-brainer for all but the most thrifty. There is a risk that you may have to upgrade the firmware of the drive going forward, but generally it's fairly simple.

It's also worth noting that the terminology surrounding these discs and drives is fairly confusing. For all practical purposes, the two "competing" DVD-Recordable formats, DVD+R and DVD-R, are the same (see next section), but they're a little more divergent in the dual-layer scene than on the single-layer side. For one thing, as of November 2004, there are no dual-layer DVD-R discs or drives that will write them; dual-layer DVD-R isn't expected to see the light of day until sometime in 2005. The dual-layer discs you *will* find are "plus" family discs, called "DVD+R DL." And to make matters more confusing, they're officially known as "double-layer" discs, even though the accepted term for DVDs with two layers has been "dual layer" ever since DVD first appeared in 1997. If you're looking for a DL-capable drive or DL media, unfortunately, you'll have to keep your eye out for all of these terms.

Is There a Difference Between DVD-R/RW and DVD+R/RW?

The biggest current difference (as of late 2004) is that there are no dual-layer DVD-R products yet available. That said, there are many drives that support DVD-R/RW and DVD+R/RW, as well as DVD+R dual-layer (usually designated as DVD+R DL). Virtually all currently shipping DVD-Recordable drives support both the plus (+) and minus (–) formats, although some of the older drives integrated into new PCs may only support one format or the other. Drives that support both single-layer standards double your media options, and improve your chances of producing a disc that will play on any given player (more on this in the next question). Since there is no price premium for drives that support both -R/RW and +R/RW, I would definitely recommend buying a drive that supports both formats, whether you're buying a single- or dual-layer recorder.

Will Discs Produced by My DVD Recorder Play on All DVD Players?

No. Compatibility appears to be improving, with some studies placing single-layer DVD-R and DVD+R compatibility well over 90 percent, but that still means that if you send your DVDs to 100 viewers, five to ten won't be able to play the disc. For this reason, when sending a disc, I always inform the recipient of the potential for compatibility issues, and tell them to contact me if this occurs.

You can minimize the risk of compatibility issues by:

- Using name-brand media. I use exclusively Verbatim and Ridata.

- Keeping the combined audio/video data rate below 8Mbps, since many players will sputter on media encoded at higher rates and burned to recordable media (go with 7Mbps to be truly conservative).

- Deliver your projects on DVD-R, *not* DVD-RW; disc/player compatibility is always better with write-once media than with rewritable media.

- Never apply paper disc labels on DVDs. Printing directly on the media with an inkjet or similar printer is fine.

I like DVD recorders that support both DVD-R/RW and DVD+R/RW because if I produce a disc in one format that won't play on a DVD player, I simply produce another using the other format. Invariably, the second disc is compatible with the player in question.

Putting Content on Your Disc

Now let's talk about the types of content you can use in your DVD productions.

What Audio and Video Formats Can I Use?

DVDs can contain video in MPEG-1 and MPEG-2 formats. Most authoring programs can input a wide variety of video formats, such as MPEG, AVI, and MOV, and convert to MPEG-1 or 2 as necessary before burning the disc.

In terms of audio, DVDs can contain an uncompressed LPCM (linear pulse code modulated, same as CD-Audio) format as well as Dolby Digital (also known as AC-3) and MPEG-2 audio compression.

Why Should I Care About Dolby Digital Audio?

In the United States, DVD players are *not* required to play back MPEG-2 audio compression, just LPCM and AC-3. While most newer DVD players can play discs with MPEG-2 audio, there's a risk that older players won't be able to decode the audio. For this reason, few if any Hollywood DVDs ship solely with MPEG-2 audio compression; they all use Dolby Digital.

If you're producing for business use, Dolby is the only viable audio compression option, though not all authoring products can output Dolby audio streams. If your authoring program doesn't support Dolby, you're at a significant disadvantage quality-wise, even if disk capacity isn't an issue. Here's why.

If you're starting with DV video, your uncompressed audio data rate may be as high as 1,500Kbps. To achieve the optimal 8Mbps bitrate for the mixed audio/video stream, you'll have to encode the video at 6,500Kbps. In contrast, with Dolby you can produce a high-quality compressed audio stream at around 200Kbps, leaving 7,800 for video, which is 20 percent higher than the maximum bitrate with PCM audio. With high-motion video, the higher bitrate could produce noticeably better quality.

The difference gets even more significant as you store more video minutes on the DVD. With two hours of video to store on a 4.7GB disc, the producer using Dolby Digital audio can encode the video to about 4,700Kbps, a challenging rate, but probably acceptable for lower-motion video. Without Dolby, however, the producer must encode to 3,300Kbps, at which point it starts to look pretty awful.

You can see why then using Dolby Digital audio is a critical feature for anyone producing DVDs for professional use.

Can I Insert Slideshows?

Yes. You can combine digital pictures and audio, and many DVD authoring programs provide dedicated slideshow creation interfaces. How the program renders the slideshow has a dramatic impact on slideshow bitrate and file size.

Some programs convert the slideshow to a video at 30 frames per second, and encode it just like any other video file. If each image in the slideshow displays for five seconds, and your average video bit rate is 7Mbps, each slide will consume 35 megabits of data (7Mbps times 5 seconds) or close to 4.4 megabytes of space on the disc.

Other programs create "true" DVD slideshows that instruct the player to display a single frame for the entire duration specified in the slideshow. Since a single frame of video might only be about 60 kilobytes in size, five seconds of video consumes 60 kilobytes on the disc. Also, if you take this approach, or avoid the compression artifacts that often accompany still images encoded into MPEG-2 format, and achieve a more crisp display.

If your productions are slideshow-intensive, and require precise bit-budgeting, find out which of the above methods your authoring program uses; otherwise your calculations will be off. If the manual or product FAQ doesn't provide the answer, build and render a 10-minute slideshow to DVD and see how much space it consumes.

Many video and DVD tools are now incorporating basic "pan and zoom" capabilities for spicing up slideshows with motion effects—think of how Ken Burns uses this technique in his documentaries. With "true" DVD slideshows, involving only MPEG-2 (I-Frame) stills, the only place you can add effects is during transitions. So if you want to pan and zoom your images, converting the slideshow to a video is your only option.

What About Text Subtitles?

The DVD specification supports up to 32 text tracks for karaoke and subtitling. But not all DVD authoring programs can insert text subtitles. See Chapter 11 for more on subtitles.

What About Multiple Audio Tracks?

The DVD specification supports up to eight tracks of digital audio, encoded in PCM, AC-3, or MPEG-2. Again, not all DVD authoring programs can insert multiple audio tracks.

By the Way, What's a VOB File?

VOB stands for Video Object. After rendering all your audio and video files into their required formats, your authoring program creates one or more VOB file, which also contain the menus along with the content. Essentially, it's your MPEG-2 video plus all the descriptive and navigational information that makes your content DVD-compatible. These are the files that are actually burned to disc.

How Do I Build My Menus?

Menus provide three basic functions. First, they provide an aesthetic introduction to the content on the disc, which is why we attempt to make our menus as attractive as possible. Second, they provide a link to the content, as in, "click this button and watch the video." Finally, menus control how the viewer navigates through the content, typically via menu-to-menu links.

In terms of aesthetics, all authoring programs include menu design capabilities, but they vary dramatically in terms of the features and design flexibility. All authoring programs provide various ways to link content to menu buttons—it's more of a mechanical function so there's little tangible difference between the programs.

Where there is significant difference is between consumer and professional authoring programs and the amount of navigational freedom each provides. If you want to create an intuitive and efficient path to your content, you're probably going to have to go for a prosumer authoring tool, which will put you above the $100 price range.

What are the Basic Design Components of a Menu?

All menus share a core set of common characteristics. Let's explore these in **Figures 8.1** and **8.2**.

Figure 8.1 is a simple DVD menu with a bitmapped image as the background. Most authoring programs supply images such as the one shown to serve as a background, or you can create and insert your own. Alternatively, you can use a solid-color background or a video background such as that shown in Figure 8.2.

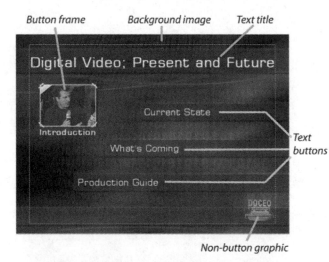

Figure 8.1.
A simple DVD menu.

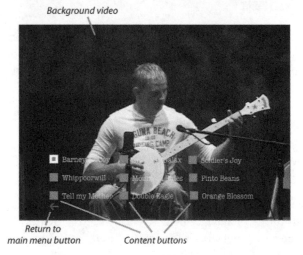

Figure 8.2.
A menu with a motion video background.

All other menu components fall neatly into two categories: buttons, which are linked components that display content or jump to another menu when clicked; and everything else. As you can see in Figure 8.1, text can be a button linking to other menus (text buttons) or simply a title that doesn't link to anything. Graphics can also be linked to content, (see the button frame on the upper left, which plays a video file when clicked), or serve as garnish, (see the logo in the bottom right corner).

All authoring programs supply text-creation and editing tools to create text titles and labels. Most also include simple drawing tools to create background boxes or circles as well as libraries of clip art you can use as buttons or additional garnish.

Most authoring programs also allow you to customize the appearance of buttons in each of their three states: Normal, Selected, and Activated. For example, in Figure 8.2, the button and text "The Wreck" is in selected state, while all other buttons are in normal state.

As the viewer clicks through the buttons using the arrow keys on the DVD remote control, each button in turn will show its selected state. When clicked, the button will display the activated state, and then play the song. Usually, you can tell you're in an activated state by color, but some programs also allow you to change graphics, underline the text, place a box around the button or similar effects. Figure 8.2 also contains a menu button that takes the viewer back to the main menu (shown on the lower left).

Figure 8.2 also shows a menu with a video background—this option is available on almost all authoring programs. Operationally, the video plays behind the menu buttons from the time the menu loads until the viewer clicks on a button. Another interesting common feature is the ability to insert an audio file, which plays until the viewer clicks on a button; you can also animate button frames, (like that shown in Figure 8.1) so that animation video audio starts playing within the frame when the menu appears.

The key point to remember about these audio and visual baubles is that they cost you both disc space and rendering time. That is, if you add a two-minute video background to your menu, that's two additional minutes of video the authoring program must encode and store on disc, extending your production time and leaving less disc space for other content.

How Do Navigational Options Vary By Program?

Navigation refers to how the viewer moves through the content on a DVD, and your ability to customize navigational structure varies greatly by program. The most flexible products—usually those costing $300 and more (with some exceptions)—allow you complete navigational flexibility, to guide your viewers as you see fit. An example of this is shown in **Figure 8.3**.

Let me set the project up for you. The videos were a composite of two interviews performed by Ken Santucci at a recent National Association of Broadcasters convention. The conversation began with the current state of the digital video market, then moved on to what new technologies were coming, and finished with some production tips.

When creating the DVD, my goal was to allow the viewer to move through the project as efficiently as possible. So I created separate menus covering each general topic we discussed, with specific button frames to launch more discrete topics. As you can see in Figure 8.3, this is called a branched menu structure because it resembles the branches of a tree.

Navigation though the title is logical and intuitive, and the viewer is never more than two clicks away from the desired content. The only negative here is that, as designer, I am in charge of creating all menu-to-menu and button-to-content links. This means more time developing and more risk of production errors. For example, when designing menus and titles from scratch, it's easy to forget to create a home button to link the viewer back to the main menu, or to forget to create the link between button and menu.

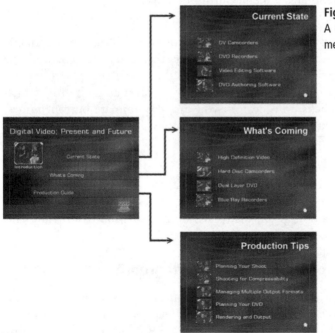

Figure 8.3.
A custom-designed, branched menu structure.

In contrast, with template-based, sequential menu designs—the only option with most consumer authoring programs—the program creates all menu-to-menu and button-to-content links automatically. All you do is choose a template and identify the desired video and chapter points, and the program does the rest. The result is shown in **Figure 8.4**.

The little white icons on the bottom right of all the menus in Figure 8.4 are links to the menu immediately before and after the current menu, as well as a home button to get you back to where you started. The authoring program created all these links automatically, as it did links to all separate videos in the project. This reduces your authoring time significantly, and helps prevent design errors.

The obvious downside is the end-user experience. All menus and videos are presented in sequential order; it's logical enough, but lacks the organization that guides the viewer through the disc, as well as the customization that might make a particular menu structure a better fit for a specific project. It's not the additional one or two clicks it takes the viewer to get to the desired content; it's the blind paging, which leaves viewers with no clue what's on the final menu page until they arrive. As you would expect, most consumer DVD authoring products in the sub-$100 price range are limited to template-based, sequential projects, which are clearly inferior to branched designs for professional use.

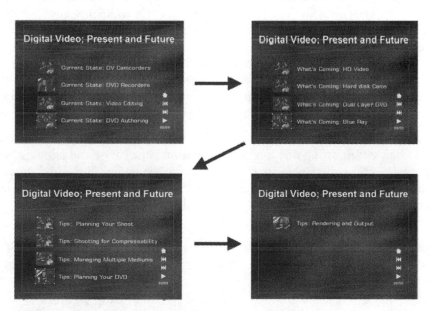

Figure 8.4. Template-based, sequential menus.

How Do I Allow the User to Jump to a Random Point in the Video File (What Are Chapter Points)?

Good question, and the current project is a perfect example. We filmed the interview live in two sessions and performed no editing, leaving two large video files to input into the DVD authoring program. Obviously, you can link to the start of any video (or slideshow for that matter), but how do you create links to sections *within* the video file? **Figure 8.5** provides the answer.

Virtually all DVD authoring programs let you create what are called "chapter points" in your videos, usually by moving to the desired frame and selecting "insert chapter point" or a similarly named function from the right-click menu. Once it's created, you can link a chapter point to any menu button just as you would with the start of the video.

Chapter points are very effective when converting long video files to DVD—in fact, virtually all Hollywood movies converted to DVD use chapter points to link movie sections to menu buttons. In addition to being simple and fast to create, chapter points within a movie don't interrupt the flow of playback from one chapter point to another.

In the video shown in Figure 8.5, for example, if the viewer started watching at the first chapter point, the movie would flow through each subsequent chapter point without interruption until that video finished playing or the viewer interrupted by clicking the DVD remote. In contrast, if you produced each section as a separate video file, and then attempted to play sequentially from file to file, the player would pause for a second or two between each separate video file, showing a black screen in the interim. Not quite the track-switch *thunk* of an 8-track tape (boy, am I dating myself), but definitely something to avoid whenever possible.

For this reason, whenever producing a video you expect viewers to watch from start to finish, outputting one long video file from your editor and adding chapter points to create discrete entry points is usually the preferred method. In fact, when working with long, sequential videos, the only reason to output separate files from your editor is if you need separate files to produce a playlist.

Figure 8.5. The chapter markers shown at the top provide specific points in the video to link to buttons on the menu.

What's a Playlist?

I thought this question was coming. Let me explain in the context of a recent project, where I shot, edited, and produced a DVD of a concert hosted by a local music association. The concert was about 60 minutes in length, consisting of 11 songs, each about three minutes long, with the rest of the time taken up by the performers chatting and telling stories.

Just to add a little context, performers were two of the surviving members of the Stoneman family, who'd played at the White House, hosted their own network television show in the '50s and '60s, and recorded at the historic 1928 Bristol sessions, which arguably launched commercial country music. They were country music before country music was cool, and for many in the audience, it was the stories—more than the music itself—that made the concert. So I wasn't about to cut the talk from the DVD.

But I did want to offer DVD viewers the ability to see just the music portion—click one button and see all 11 songs in a row, minus the stories. The answer? Playlists. Briefly, playlists (called "stories" in some programs), let you link together noncontiguous chunks of DVD content and combine them into a sequential presentation.

Without playlists, I'd have had to create and render a separate video file containing just the songs in my video editor and add that video to the DVD, piling on another 30 minutes of video to an already crowded DVD. In contrast, playlists work with content already inserted into the project, and thus add minimal extra content to the disc.

However, playlists work differently in different programs. Some authoring programs start playing at a chapter point in the video and automatically stop playing at the next chapter point. As shown in **Figure 8.6**, to prepare the converted video for the playlist, I created a chapter point at the start of every song, and then added a chapter point at the end of each song, basically when the applause died down. For example, "Barney McCoy" is the start of a song, "Barney end" is the end of the song.

Basically, to create the playlist, I created a list of the chapter points (called story markers in the authoring program I used, as shown in **Figure 8.7**) that marked the beginning of each song. During playback, this list instructs the DVD player to start the song, exit at the next chapter point, then re-enter at the next designated chapter point, the start of the next song.

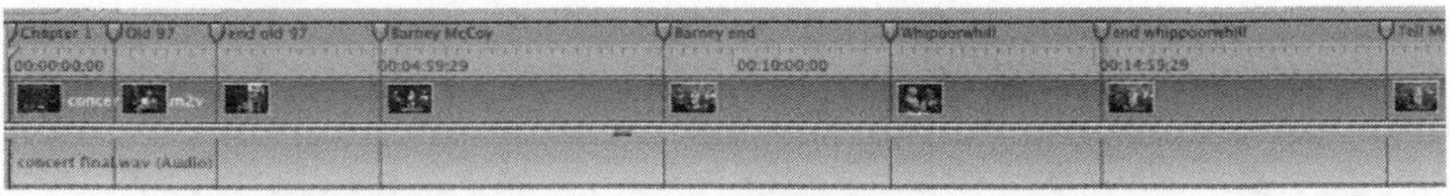

Figure 8.6. Creating end chapter points to create a playlist.

No.	Story Markers	Running Time
1	Old 97 Entry	00:01:24;02
2	Barney McCoy Entry	00:05:20;14
3	Whipoorwhill Entry	00:08:16;20
4	Tell Mother Entry	00:12:19;11
5	girl galax Entry	00:14:24;00
6	Mountain blues Entry	00:16:55;19
7	double eagle Entry	00:20:19;25
8	somebodys waiting Entry	00:23:24;06
9	Soldier's Joy Entry	00:25:15;07
10	pinto beans Entry	00:27:23;16
11	orange blossom Entry	00:29:58;02

Figure 8.7.
The playlist is a simple list of starting points.

When watching the playlist from DVD, the viewer experiences about a one-second delay between songs, but that's expected, because the viewer knows the video is jumping from song to song. However, since I used chapter points to create the links for the playlist, viewers watching the concert from start to finish would experience smooth, uninterrupted playback.

It may sound minor, but the key feature offered by this program was the ability for a playlist to exit at a chapter point. Not all programs can do this. If this is the case for you; and you create a playlist that includes a chapter point within a video file, the video will play from the chapter point until the end of the video file.

Clearly, this wouldn't work if the concert video was one long file accessed via chapter points. Applying this to my project, I would have to split the concert into 22 separate files—one containing a song, the next containing the post-song discussion, then another song, more discussion, and so on.

Then I would link the songs together into a playlist that simply pointed to each song in sequential order. During playback, the viewer would experience short breaks between the songs, just as with the other technique, which would be fine.

However, because I had to break the concert into separate video files, viewers choosing to watch the entire concert sequentially would experience a short break during each transition between songs. At the end of the applause to "Barney

McCoy," for example, there would be a short pause until the performers started chatting, then a short break before the next song started. This would not sit well with the viewer, because the breaks come between linear segments of the concert, and are clearly artificial.

Going forward, I'm sure most programs will boost their playlist functions with the ability to exit at a chapter point. If your program doesn't support this feature, you'll have to balance the value of the playlist against the value of uninterrupted playback of the sequential video. If you don't expect many viewers to watch the video, from start to finish, breaking your video into the pieces necessary to support a playlist won't be an issue. But if you're expecting sequential viewing, you'll have a much tougher decision.

How Do I Control Viewer Navigation?

Menu structure is a major issue, but there are other factors involved in controlling how your viewers navigate through the content on the disc. When planning a DVD, ask yourself the following questions to fine-tune the user experience.

(Note that while most $300-plus authoring programs include the features discussed here, playlists and many other sophisticated navigational capabilities are simply not available authoring program under $100.)

What Happens When the Viewer Inserts the Disc (First Play Video)?

When you play a Hollywood DVD, the first thing you typically see is the friendly FBI warning describing the penalties for copying the DVD. The technical term for this is the First Play video, and many authoring programs allow you to add a First Play video to the DVD. This is a completely artistic decision, with one caveat—if you insert a First Play video, it's usually best to keep it short, generally around a minute or so, since your viewers will be forced to watch it every time they play the disc.

If you opt not to include a First Play video, the first menu in the project (also called the Top menu) should appear after the viewer inserts the disc. Some programs automatically assign Top menu status to the first menu in the project; with others, you'll specifically have to identify a menu as the Top menu.

If you do insert a First Play video into your project, you may have to designate what happens after the video finishes playing. Typically, you accomplish this by assigning the Top menu as the "end action" for the First Play video. I'll explain this further two questions down.

What Happens if No One Clicks Anything (Menu Timeout)?

OK, the viewer is now at the Top menu, either because there was no First Play video, or because it's already played through. Now you have to plan what happens if no buttons are clicked. This is often a concern for discs produced for trade shows, kiosks, or other unattended uses (not to mention inexperienced DVD viewers). In the event of a power outage at the show, or a nontechnical user running the computer or player, you want the DVD to start playing the desired content automatically after a few moments.

The mechanism used to start the content playing is typically a menu timeout. You set duration, as shown in **Figure 8.8**, and then enter an End Action to tell the DVD where to go after the timeout period. In Figure 8.8, I'm telling the DVD to wait one minute, then jump to the menu Current State and activate the DV Camcorders button, which will start that video playing.

If we didn't assign the menu a duration and End Action, the menu would remain onscreen until a viewer clicked a button, which is also acceptable for many applications. If you include a video background or audio file, you can typically have these files play again and again (called looping) until the viewer interrupts by clicking.

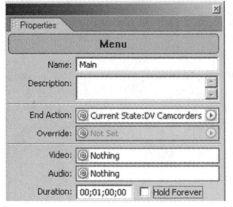

Figure 8.8.
Setting a menu duration and End Action so the content on the DVD automatically starts playing.

What Happens Next (End Action)?

I've mentioned end actions twice, so let's explore the subject more fully. Basically, the End Action is where the viewer goes next, either after a video or slideshow finishes playing, or if viewer interrupts playback, or a menu simply times out. For example, in Figure 8.8, after the one-minute menu timeout, the DVD will play the DV Camcorders video in the Current State menu. If you check Figure 8.3, you'll see that this is the first video in the first menu with content.

Even though your flexibility regarding end actions is very limited in consumer programs, with most prosumer packages you can create an End Action that jumps to any menu or other content in the DVD. If the primary application for the DVD is unattended operation, you'd link all videos via sequential end actions, and then link the last video to the first video to start the loop anew.

With most other DVDs, you may want to choose a different behavior. For example, in my interview DVD, which is not really intended for unattended operation, I wanted the viewer to play through all the videos *on each content menu* and then return to the Top menu. I accomplish this by setting a return-to-menu flag after the video from the fourth chapter point finishes as shown in **Figure 8.9**.

The basic rule of thumb is, you ask the same question—"what happens next?"— for each menu and video or slideshow included in the project, going from button to button, menu to menu. When the end action is to send your viewer to a menu, you of course must revisit the question "what happens if no one clicks anything?" and then deal with the timeout issue.

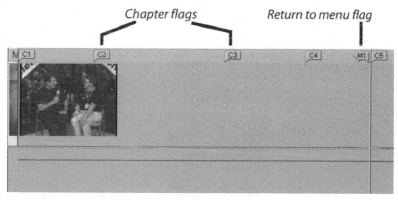

Chapter flags   *Return to menu flag*

Figure 8.9. Setting a return-to-menu flag to go back to the menu after the video from the fourth chapter point stops playing.

What About Menu-to-Menu Links?

If you look at Figure 8.3, you'll notice that all three content menus have little home buttons on the bottom right, which the viewer clicks to return to the Top menu. In addition, I could have inserted links on each menu with videos to the other menu with videos—just as most Web pages contain links to other pages on the site. I chose not to, forcing the viewer to return to the main menu to view other content pages. However, if you feel the inclusion of menu-to-menu links would enhance the viewing experience for your viewers, by all means include them.

How Do I Fit All This on Disc?

Good question, if not *the* question. Unfortunately, getting all your content to fit on disc is often harder than you think, and certainly harder than it needs to be.

Let's quickly review. You've added menus, audio, video, and slideshows to your disc. If your authoring software gives you a Dolby audio compression option, you'll almost certainly use it, so that data rate is fixed. This leaves the data rate of the video as the most significant variable you need to adjust to fit the contents on disc.

Some programs figure out the required video data rate internally, and automatically compress the video to the bitrate necessary to fit it all on disc. Obviously, this is the preferred approach. Other programs, however, force you to calculate the necessary rate, though, generally, not without some assistance.

Specifically, when starting a project, you'll usually set the project encoding parameters, using a control such as that shown in **Figure 8.10**. Then, as you add content to the project, you'll see the contents accumulate in some kind of meter, such as the one shown in **Figure 8.11**.

Figure 8.10.
Setting project encoding parameters.

Twenty minutes available   Nine minutes over

Figure 8.11. A capacity meter that tells you how much room remains (on the left), or when you're out of space (on the right).

If you exceed the capacity of the disc, you have two choices: lower the video bitrate or delete content. This type of scrambling occurs more often than you think, and why I recommend encoding all assets as part of the final rendering and burning process.

Specifically, if you're working with a separate video editor and authoring program, don't encode into MPEG-2 format when outputting from the editor, because you may later discover that the bitrate was too high or too low. Rather, output in DV format and encode as part of the final rendering process.

Similarly, some authoring programs let you encode video files into MPEG-2 format as an interim production step. Unless your disc contents are absolutely nailed down, however, you may find yourself having to encode again to a different bitrate. Again, I can't recommend enough waiting until the project is finished, and the optimal bitrate conclusive, before you encode your video.

What About Bit Budgeting?

Bit budgeting is for Type A personalities who want to know how much video will fit on their discs and at what rate before they start authoring. Not a bad thing (hey, I'm definitely Type A), but a bit difficult to explain in the abstract, because bit-budgeting is both project- and authoring program-specific. Let's review some general principles.

The first principle is that all content counts. It's not just video, audio, and slideshows; it's all of that plus audio menus, video menus, animated button frames, multiple audio tracks for languages, and multiple subtitle tracks. To perform a precise bit-budget allocation, you need to know the following:

- The bitrate used for audio menus (generally the bitrate applied to other audio files).

- The bitrate the program uses for video menus (generally, the bitrate applied to video files).

- How the program encodes slideshows (whether it converts the slideshow into a video file or displays the still images).

- The bitrate used for language tracks (generally, the bitrate applied to other audio files).

The second principle is that authoring programs typically can't use the same asset multiple times. For example, suppose you have four menus in your project and use the same two-minute video behind each menu. In a perfect world, the authoring program would encode and store the video once on disc and tell the DVD player to play that file behind each menu. Unfortunately, most authoring programs don't work that way; they produce the video file four times and store all four files on the disc.

Sounds Too Complex; How About Some Examples?

Sounds good to me. **Table 8.2** shows the bitrate for five projects, ranging in size from 60 minutes to 120 minutes. Included are encoding parameters for programs both with Dolby encoding (at 192Kbps) and with LPCM output (at 44.1kHz, 16-bit stereo, or 1,408Kbps).

Table 8.2. Video-only bitrates for five project sizes using Dolby and PCM encoding.

Disc capacity	4.7GB	4.7GB	4.7GB	4.7GB	4.7GB
Minutes of video	120	105	90	75	60
Video-only bitrate (Dolby)	4700	5400	6400	7700	7808
Video-only bitrate (LPCM)	3500	4200	5200	6500	6592

Let me add a couple of explanatory notes. First, the combined audio/video bitrate on any project burned to a DVD-Recordable disc should never exceed 8Mbps, and I've limited the video bitrates for both 60-minute projects to reflect this. Put another way; if your project has less than 60 minutes of video, bit budgeting isn't really an issue.

Second, if you're using MPEG-2 audio compression at a similar 192Kbps rate, the results will obviously be the same as those shown in Table 8.2. That said, I don't recommend using MPEG-2 audio for discs built for business use because of the compatibility issues I've already described.

Third, these numbers assume only one audio track and no audio or video menus. If you are including these in your project, you'll have to factor this content into the equation.

Back on the Farm, How Do I Build This Thing?

OK, we've gotten most of the tough planning issues out of the way, and imported and added chapter points to our video. Now let's get back to work and finish this project. First up is linking our buttons to content and other menus.

Linking Your Content and Menus

Generally, there are two ways to link buttons to either menus or content. Most programs use drag and drop, as shown in **Figure 8.12**. Typically, you grab the chapter point or menu you want to link to with your mouse, drag it onto the button, and release, usually guided by symbols such as the plus sign visible in Figure 8.12.

Alternatively, some programs use right-click menus to allow you to choose the target video and chapter point, as shown in **Figure 8.13**; it's less visual, but gets the job done.

Once you identify your preferred method of linking, link all buttons to their targets. The next step is to preview your DVD and check your work.

Figure 8.12. Dragging the target into the button frame to create the link.

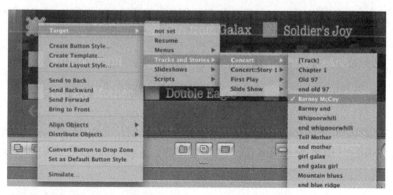

Figure 8.13. Selecting the button target via right mouse-click commands.

How do I Preview my DVD?

All DVD authoring programs allow you to simulate the playback of your DVD in preview mode or a similar with simulated controls containing all the controls normally found on a DVD remote. This is demonstrated in **Figure 8.14**.

Using this control, test all project links to verify their accuracy—tedious but critical. For example, while some programs automatically check to make sure a button is *linked*, there's no way the program can ensure it's linked to the *right* target. There's also no automatic way to verify that chapter points are set to the right location. During preview, you'll also discover whether all menus have links back to the main menu (otherwise, you'll be left hanging), and check that all menu timeouts and end actions are working as you planned.

Figure 8.14.
Run a DVD playback simulator to check your project.

Note that some programs offer a view that displays the target of each button on the menu, as shown in **Figure 8.15**. This is a really helpful to quickly identify mistakes.

As you move up in price, authoring programs offer increasing ranges of error detection, from "orphan menus" that aren't linked to any other menu, to unlinked buttons, missing assets, and far, far beyond. As mentioned before, however, these functions can't detect when you've made a mistake and linked to the wrong content, so you're still going to have to perform your own comprehensive preview and manual error-checking.

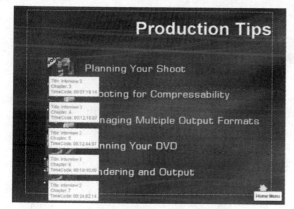

Figure 8.15.
In this view, the menu displays the targets of all buttons.

Time to Burn

At this point, it's time to burn, which is generally a fairly mechanical option, especially if you're already selected your video encoding parameters. **Figure 8.16** shows a typical DVD burning screen. If you're concerned with options such as copy protection and region encoding, check the manual of your authoring program.

If you plan to make multiple copies of the DVD, have the program create the necessary files and store them to disc before burning; that way you won't have to re-render the entire project to create another copy. At this stage, most programs will advise you if you have too much content for the disc using the current encoding settings, which isn't a problem here.

Figure 8.16.
Burning options are generally fairly limited.

Finishing Touches

I don't know about you, but after I've spent hours working on a DVD, scribbling the title with a permanent Sharpie on the disc just doesn't cut it. Fortunately, the cost of tricking out your disc and jewel case covers has really dropped over the last few years.

The most critical tool in your arsenal is a printer capable of printing directly on the surface of your DVD blanks. I've used the Epson Stylus R200 (about $99 direct) shown in **Figure 8.17** as a disc and label printer offering great results; the ink consumption also has been quite reasonable. The unit has individual ink cartridges, which you can replace when they run out. This is more efficient than cartridges that contain multiple colors which you have to replace when *any* color runs out.

You'll need to get special "printable" DVDs, which generally come with a plain white surface. Fortunately these are now widely available from many vendors including Verbatim and Ridata, and only slightly more expensive than blank DVDs with nonprintable surfaces. Once again, I recommend strongly against using paper labels on DVDs—it really hurts their playback compatibility.

Figure 8.17.
The Epson Stylus R200, just finishing another printable DVD.

To create your artwork, Epson includes its own Print CD software, which can import a background image and provides a good range of drawing and text-entry tools. As you can see in **Figure 8.18**, I used a screen shot from the DVD as the label, moving it about strategically so the hole in the middle of the disc wouldn't obscure anything critical.

Figure 8.18.
Preparing a disc label using Epson's Print CD software.

Epson's software doesn't create jewel-case covers so I turned to Verbatim for print supplies, software, and (of course) blank printable media. The software is surprisingly feature-rich, with support for tables, background images, and multiple themes, and made short work of the multiple jewel-case covers shown in **Figure 8.19**. You can see the Verbatim DVD/CD label kit in the background.

If you're delivering your DVDs to a client, whether internal, external, or family, I definitely recommend investing $100 in a label printer. These professional labels make an awesome first impression for any project.

Figure 8.19.
Printed materials like these help make a great first impression.

In the Workbook

The workbook for this chapter includes:

- A description of the program's navigational controls.

- A description of the program's menu timeout, end action, and playlist capabilities.

- A step-by-step workflow for producing the interview DVD shown in Figure 8.3, complete with menu creation, linking, previewing, and burning.

Go to *www.doceo.com/DV101.html* for a list of currently supported products.

Chapter 9:
Using Video in Presentations

Incorporating video into presentations is the great grassroots business use of video—not quite as sexy as DVD or as hip as streaming, but the bread and butter of road warriors around the globe. In this chapter, we describe how to insert video into PowerPoint (for Windows and Mac) and Apple Keynote.

As you would expect, each program has its own peculiarities. There are also red flags to be aware of, especially if I've been creating a presentation on one computer and playing it from another.

Let's start with Keynote: you can embed the video file into the presentation itself, so wherever the presentation goes, the video file goes. This makes it simple to create a presentation on one computer and display it on another.

In contrast, you can't embed video files into PowerPoint. The PowerPoint project files may stay smaller, but also complicates transferring your presentation to a different computer. Not only must you transfer the video file(s) to the target computer, but they also must reside in the exact same folder on that computer.

To make things as easy as possible, I create all presentations in a drive called c:\apresent on my video workstation in the lab, and copy all video files into that folder before linking them inside PowerPoint. Then, I transfer the files to a similarly named subdirectory on my laptop.

Why c:\apresent instead of just c:\present? Because the odds are that during the presentation I'll have to find the folder to locate a demo file or two, and if I use c:\apresent, the folder will generally fall at the top of the list in Windows Explorer, and therefore be easier to find.

My other prepresentation essential is to create a desktop shortcut to the PowerPoint or Keynote file itself. This way, if either program crashes—quite likely since I've usually got multiple video players and two or three authoring, editing, or encoding programs open at the same time—it takes just one click to get it started again.

Finally, if your presentation is displayed on a projector, test its performance on the same projector beforehand if possible. If you can't, remember that most projectors are still limited to 1,024x768 or even 800x600 resolution, and projects developed on 1,280x1024 and especially 1,920x1,200 will look vastly different at these lower resolutions.

Inserting Video into PowerPoint for Windows

Housekeeping issues aside, let's examine our integration options, starting with PowerPoint for Windows. Just for the record, and in the absence of other considerations (such as cross-platform delivery), I use 640x480 Windows Media video files, encoded to about 4Mbps, for most Windows-based PowerPoint use.

Insert Action Button (All Video Types)

The Insert Action button gives you the broadest range of integration options, including Windows Media, QuickTime, RealVideo, MPEG-1 and 2, and MPEG-4. You start by clicking the Insert Action button as shown in **Figure 9.1**.

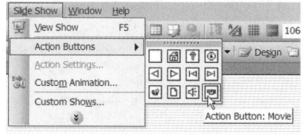

Figure 9.1.
Action buttons can insert any program into PowerPoint, including RealVideo and QuickTime.

This in turn creates a button on the PowerPoint page—presenters click to launch a separate application such as the QuickTime, RealPlayer, or Windows Media Player, which loads your target video file (**Figure 9.2**). Once PowerPoint launches the player program, you control the operations exactly as you would normally during playback.

This is your best option if you have multiple files to present from a single page, as both the other options use embedded windows, limiting you in terms of real-estate, to two or three videos at most. It's also your only option if you're attempting to play either RealVideo or QuickTime video files without a separate third-party plug-in.

Insert Object

Figure 9.2. Your three PowerPoint integration alternatives.

Insert Movies and Sounds

Insert Action Button

Linking files in this manner is fairly simple. You start by clicking Slide Show > Action Button > Movie, which turns your pointer into a cross you use to draw the button on the slide. Once you finish, PowerPoint launches an Action Setting dialog (**Figure 9.3**). Click the Hyperlink to Radio button and then click the adjoining list box and select Other File. PowerPoint opens a standard File Open dialog, which you can use to navigate to the correct folder to click on the target file. Click OK to close the Action Settings window.

I usually test my links each time by running the slideshow and then clicking the button, since it's easy enough to mistype a file name or location. Also, if you're transferring your presentation to another computer, beware of applications loaded in other locations.

For example, Real used to install the Player at c:\real\ before they got with the program and started using c:\program files\real. But this created a new problem. Once, I'd installed the new player (which uninstalled the old player) at the right location, none of my links would work—something I found out in real time onstage. So, my motto is test, test, test, and tell your roving presenters to do the same.

Figure 9.3.
Select the Run program and click the Browse button to locate the application to run.

Insert Movie (MPEG, Windows Media, AVI Files)

The next alternative is to select the Insert > Movies and Sounds > Movie from File demonstrated in **Figure 9.4**. This launches an Insert Movie dialog used to navigate to and select the video file. PowerPoint then lets you choose whether to launch the file automatically when the slide opens, or by clicking on the embedded movie window. With both alternatives, you click on the window to stop playback.

The video window you create in PowerPoint is easy to resize, but you have to use the aspect ratio of the video itself, to avoid distortion. If you right-click on the movie window, you can select Edit Movie Object to loop the video, zoom it to full screen, or rewind it after completion (this is shown in **Figure 9.5**). You can also create a Custom Animation for the start or end of playback.

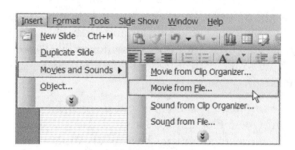

Figure 9.4.
For Windows Media, MPEG, and AVI files, you can select the Insert Movie option.

Figure 9.5.
Movie Options for videos inserted using the Insert Movie option.

This mechanism works for Windows Media, MPEG, and AVI files, but not for QuickTime or Real. The only negative is the lack of onscreen-player options; basically, all you can do is click the video to stop and start playback. I prefer the control enabled by the next alternative, which is Inserting an Object.

Fortunately this alternative does allow you to apply PowerPoint effects to your videos, such as fading the video from black. To access these effects, right-click the video window and choose Custom Animations. Then click the Add Effect Button, which will appear in the upper right corner of your screen, and select Entrance > Fade (shown in **Figure 9.6**). If Fade is not listed, or you want to see a greater range of options, click More Effects on the bottom of the menu.

Object Linking (MPEG, Windows Media, AVI Files)

When Microsoft developed Windows Media Player, it created both a standalone application and an object that other applications could link to and functionally access. Briefly, an object is a small program with a well-defined function (such as playing video) and programming interface—both making it simple for other developers to use and access from whatever program they are using. With object support within Media Player, any developer who wants to add video to an application can support object linking, rather than write a video application from scratch.

To put this functionality into use, choose Insert > Insert Object, which opens the Insert Object dialog. You then scroll down the list until you find the Windows Media Player (**Figure 9.7**). Select it and press OK, and PowerPoint will display a freely resizable movie window, complete with controls such as Stop, Start, volume adjustments, and a slider bar for moving through the video.

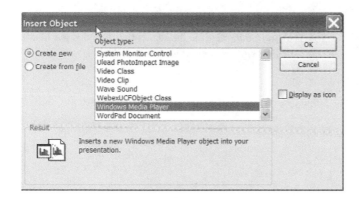

Figure 9.7.
Insert Object gives you the most control over playback options.

Right-click on the window and select Properties, and you'll see a dialog such as that shown in **Figure 9.8**.

Click Custom on top of the dialog to launch the Windows Media Player Properties dialog, which includes a browse button so you can locate your file, along with other layout, playback, and volume settings (**Figure 9.9**).

The Advanced Tab includes controls for invoking scripts, so playback can also launch your browser to a specific Web site. This is also the feature you would use to launch SAMI closed-captioned text files (I'll cover this in detail in Chapter 11).

I really like the control provided by object linking. Although it's a little more complicated than other methods and can't be used with either Real or QuickTime files, it produces the most professional-looking work.

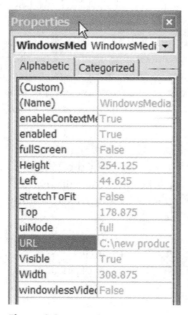

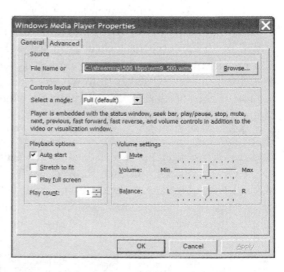

Figure 9.9. Here are the key controls for Windows Media Player when you insert video via object linking.

Figure 9.8.
Click Custom to see video object properties, organized either alphabetically or by category.

Creating Links in Your Video

If your embedded videos are long, it's often helpful to provide direct access to key segments so your presenters can jump directly to the critical area and skip over unnecessary footage. For example, wouldn't it be great to insert direct links into a 30-minute marketing video that would allow sales reps to go directly to the first frame of segments showing testimonials, Return on Investment, competition, and the like?

This is simple with Windows Media files. When you download Microsoft's Windows Media Encoder (available here: *www.microsoft.com/windows/windows-media/9series/encoder/default.aspx*), the setup routine automatically installs a utility called the Windows Media File Editor. Load your file into the File Editor (**Figure 9.10**) and then move to the start of a key segment, using either the slider bar beneath the video window or the start and pause controls (the play button converts to pause after playback starts).

Then, click Markers to open the dialog shown in **Figure 9.11**. Click Add, type the name, and press OK, and File Editor will create the marker at the current playback location in the video file. Then press OK to return to the main screen to move to another key segment. To accelerate your work, you can scan the video file in advance, noting the timecodes for all markers, and create them all at once.

During playback, your presenters can jump directly to these key segments by right-clicking and choosing File Markers, as shown in **Figure 9.12**. This can be a huge timesaver during high-pressure presentations.

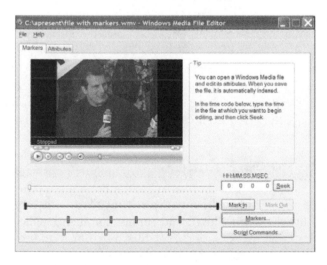

Figure 9.10.
Use the File Editor to add markers allowing your presenters to jump directly to key segments.

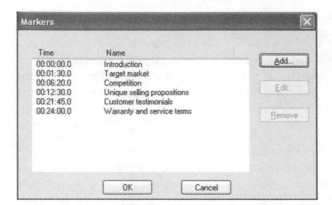

Figure 9.11.
Insert markers at key points in your video file for better access segments during playback.

Figure 9.12.
File markers let your presenters get right to the point when working with longer videos.

Remember that videos embedded using Object Linking can jump to file markers during playback, but not those embedded using the Insert Movie method. If you use the Insert Action technique, the video is played in Media Player, so you can access file markers.

Inserting Video into PowerPoint:Mac

You have two options when inserting video files into PowerPoint:Mac—one easy, one hard. The easy way is to use the Insert Movies and Sounds command, which allows you to bring in QuickTime, MPEG, and AVI files, but not Windows Media Video files.

The hard way is to insert a hyperlink to a Windows Media video or RealVideo file, which only works if you have RealPlayer and/or Windows Media Player for OSX installed. It's hard because unless you configure PowerPoint to run the presentation in a window, as detailed below, PowerPoint will exit the slideshow when you click the hyperlink and run either player.

Interestingly, MPEG-2 is the only video format that you can play from *within a window* in PowerPoint for Windows, PowerPoint:Mac, and Keynote, making it the *lingua franca* for cross-platform presentations. Fortunately, MPEG-2 holds up quite well at higher data rates (like 4Mbps), so as long as you have the disk space on all computers, your video quality should not be affected.

If you're producing videos for Macintosh use only, I recommend you encode them to QuickTime, using the Sorenson Video 3 codec. Encode at 640x480 resolution and at about 70 to 80KB/sec, which translates to around 5.6 to 6.4Mbps.

Insert Movies and Sounds

Start by clicking Insert > Movies and Sounds from PowerPoint:Mac's main menu (**Figure 9.13**). Using the Insert Movie dialog, select the target file.

Figure 9.13.
Inserting a movie into PowerPoint:Mac.

PowerPoint will give you the option to play the video once you enter the slide (**Figure 9.14**); otherwise you'll have to click the video window to play it. Choose the desired option and PowerPoint inserts the video file at near full screen. Size and position the video window as you would any graph (or text object for that matter) into PowerPoint.

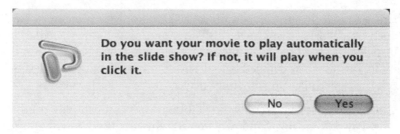

Figure 9.14. Choose the desired option in this dialog.

Now it's time to start configuring the video file. Click View > Toolbars > Movie to open the Movie Toolbar shown in **Figure 9.15**.

You can use the Insert Movie command as the starting point to insert your next video file. Click Play to start the video playing in design mode, and Show Controller to display the player controls and slider bar located on the bottom of the video and shown in **Figure 9.16**. You can set a poster frame—the frame that appears in the movie window before the video starts playing—by dragging the controller to the target frame and clicking Set Poster Frame. These controls don't appear when you play the slideshow in PowerPoint; they're just to help you work with the file when creating the slideshow.

Clicking Loop will play the video file within the slide until you click the video window to stop playback, a nice option for kiosks and other unattended presentations. Click Format Picture to expose PowerPoint's regular formatting controls for resizing, positioning, and otherwise changing the appearance of the video frame.

In the PowerPoint Preferences window, General Tab, there's a Movie Options button, which when clicked, will reveal the screen shown in **Figure 9.17**.

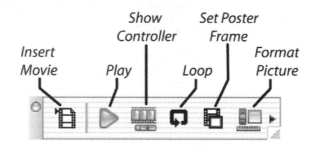

Figure 9.15. PowerPoint:Mac's Movie Toolbar.

Figure 9.16.
Use the controller to select a poster frame.

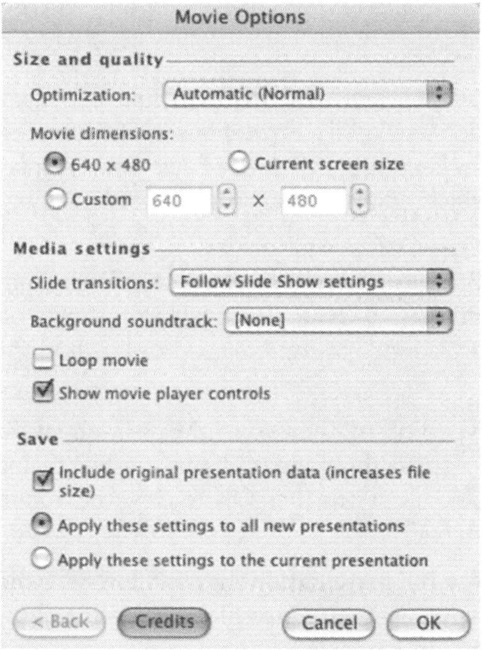

Figure 9.17.
PowerPoint:Mac's Movie Options.

Despite making sure that the Show movie player controls checkbox was enabled, PowerPoint:Mac did not insert player controls in any of the inserted movies, whether QuickTime or MPEG-2. Instead, when playing the videos in Slide Show mode, we clicked the movie frame to start playback, and clicked it again to stop playback.

Bear in mind that although it looks like the Save controls on the bottom of the screen (include original presentation data) would store the video file in the PowerPoint presentation file, it didn't in our tests. There's always a chance that our results are specific to our computer, so if you want to show the player controls with your inserted movies or store the video file with the PowerPoint presentation, give these controls a try.

Insert Hyperlink

PowerPoint:Mac lets you create a hyperlink from any text or image object in a slide to any external file. When you click the link in Slide Show mode, PowerPoint will run the program necessary to play the file, such as Media Player or Real Player, and load the file into the program. From there, you play the file as normal.

As we've discussed already, if you run an external program while playing a PowerPoint presentation in normal Slide Show mode, PowerPoint closes the presentation. To keep the presentation open, you must switch the PowerPoint display from full screen to window mode, which changes the controls used to move through the slide show.

Start by clicking Slide Show > Action Buttons > Movie (**Figure 9.18**). PowerPoint will convert the cursor to a plus sign you drag to create the movie icon shown on the left in **Figure 9.19**, and will open the Action Settings screen also shown in the figure.

In the Action Settings dialog, Click Hyperlink to: then go to the drop-down list box and choose Other File. PowerPoint opens the standard Choose a File dialog that you can use to choose the target video file. Then click OK to close the Action Settings dialog, and the hyperlink is set.

Now you have to tell PowerPoint to play the presentation in a window to avoid shutting down the presentation when you play your video file. Click Slide Show > Set Up Show to open the dialog shown in **Figure 9.20**.

Click the Browsed by an individual (window) checkbox and then OK to close the dialog. Note that when you're playing a presentation in this window mode, clicking on a slide does not advance to the next slide. Instead, you have to use your right arrow key to move forwards, and the left arrow key to move backwards.

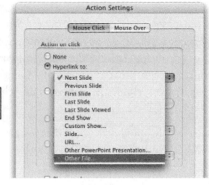

Figure 9.18. Inserting a Movie Action Button.

Figure 9.19. Choosing the file that will play when a viewer clicks the button.

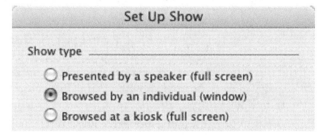

Figure 9.20. Playing the presentation in a window.

When you select Slide Show mode, and click the movie button, PowerPoint:Mac attempts to run the program required to play the selected file. Before doing so, however, it will open the warning shown in **Figure 9.21**. Though the PowerPoint:Mac help file tells you that you can disable this message by disabling macro virus protection in the General Preferences dialog (click PowerPoint > Preferences, then the General tab), this didn't work in our tests (PowerPoint:Mac Service Release 1).

Click OK, however, and the program should run with the file loaded (**Figure 9.22**). From there, you can use the normal controls to play the video file.

Apple Keynote

Keynote can play QuickTime and MPEG files in a simple embedded window. You can drag and drop the file into the slide or choose Edit > Place > Choose to browse and select the file. Once the file is inserted, you can resize the video window by clicking and dragging any edge, and drag the frame to any location in the slide.

Click the Inspector icon atop the Keynote interface to open the Inspector (**Figure 9.23**). You can drag the Poster Frame slider to display a different poster frame, control whether the file plays once or repeats continuously, and adjust volume. Note that you'll see the player controls shown on the Inspector control when you're creating the slideshow, but they do not appear *in* the slideshow. Also, you can't stop video playback in presentation mode without closing the slideshow and reverting back to design mode.

When saving the presentation file, Keynote gives you the option to save the movie files within the presentation, which is very useful when moving the presentation from one computer to another. This worked well in our tests.

Chapter 10:
Streaming with Producer for PowerPoint

OK, who out there has created a presentation in PowerPoint and then travelled somewhere far away to present it? Hmmm, many hands showing. I thought so.

OK, now how many people have travelled to multiple places to give the *same* PowerPoint presentation? Hmmm, even more hands. Well, unless travel is a bonus for you, this is your chapter.

Here we'll run through how to use Microsoft's free Producer for PowerPoint 2003 to create a presentation, complete with video and PowerPoint slides, then package it up for placing on a CD-ROM, Web site, or intranet server. You can also add Web pages and digital pictures, trim and split your videos, and even add special effects, though obviously these may degrade the compressed quality of your video (Go back to Chapter 6 for more on that). Producer is a great tool for training, communications, marketing. and sales— basically, any activity for which you've already created and given a PowerPoint presentation.

I used Producer for PowerPoint to create an explanation of the materials covered in the Delivering Digital Video class I teach for the University of Wisconsin-Madison, culminating in the presentation shown in **Figure 10.1**. On the upper right is the PowerPoint slide, and beneath the player on the left are slide titles the viewer can click and jump to. The viewer can also use the two double-arrow buttons beneath the video window to jump 10 seconds backwards and forwards.

At a high level, to create a Producer presentation, you videotape the presenter giving the presentation, either live or in the studio. You then capture or import the video (or just the audio, if desired) into Producer, import the PowerPoint slides, and synchronize them to the video. There are a few design options, such as template and font size, but overall the process is straightforward and efficient.

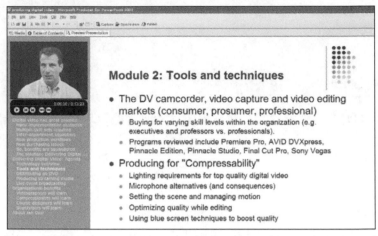

Figure 10.1. A finished presentation from Producer for PowerPoint.

Where to Get Producer for PowerPoint

Producer for PowerPoint is a free download; you can read more about the program and download it here: *www.microsoft.com/office/powerpoint/producer/prodinfo/default.mspx*. Of course, there ain't no such thing as a free lunch, even from Mother Microsoft, so you will need to have purchased either PowerPoint 2002 or 2003 to use it. You'll also need a PC with a 400mHz or faster processor, 128MB RAM or more, an 800x600-capable monitor and graphics card, and Windows 2000 Professional, XP Home, XP Professional, or XP Tablet Editions.

I'll assume that you've met the basic requirements, downloaded the program, and installed it. By default, you run the program by clicking Start > Programs > Microsoft Office > Microsoft Producer for PowerPoint 2003.

Creating Your Presentation

If you're creating a presentation to stream at low bitrates, you should film the video to make it low bitrate-friendly. As you can see from Figure 10.1, I'm shooting against a black screen, a technique for producing high-quality, low bitrate video discussed back in Chapter 6.

Choosing a Template

Producer includes a wizard interface that simplifies the process immensely, especially for your first few presentations. So let's start there. With Producer running, choose File > New Presentation Wizard to open the wizard. The initial screen is simply informational, so click Next to open the presentation template window shown in **Figure 10.2**.

Figure 10.2. Choosing your template.

Templates are visual containers that allow you to package your content differently. It may seem like just another of the many decisions in the wizard, template choice is critical. For example, over and above appearance, your template choice dictates the ultimate resolution of the video window, and whether the PowerPoint slides and HTML pages are resizable by the viewer. In Figure 10.2, I've selected the template with a 320x240 video window with resizable slide area, which will expand to fit the size of the viewer's screen.

You can change templates during the course of the presentation; perhaps showing only video during the introduction, then switching to video or even audio only along with your PowerPoint slides during the main presentation. The user will experience a short stoppage of the video while the templates are changing, but otherwise it works fairly well.

The template I chose includes video and PowerPoint slides, but there are templates for audio-only presentations, Web page presentations, and the like. Make sure you choose a template that includes the types of content you plan to use, and nothing more. For example, don't choose a template with HTML if you don't plan to add Web links.

Click each template on the left and Producer will display a description on the bottom and a preview on the right. After choosing a template, click Next to customize font and background color options (not shown).

A quick note on font size. The default is 12 points, which is highly readable, but only allows room for about 30 letters in each slide description. I needed longer descriptions in my titles, so I chose a 10-point font. You can change the template and adjust font sizes later, once you've previewed.

After customizing your font, click Next again to add the information that appears on the title of your presentation before the content starts to play. Then click Next to start loading your content.

Loading Your Content

Nothing exotic about bringing assets into Producer; operation is still-wizard driven and straightforward. First you'll import still images along with your PowerPoint project (not shown), then you either capture or insert your video files.

Note that you can choose multiple files to load, and Producer will place them sequentially on the timeline in the order shown in the files box. If you have multiple files, you can use the Move Up and Move Down buttons (not activated in **Figure 10.3**) to reorder the files.

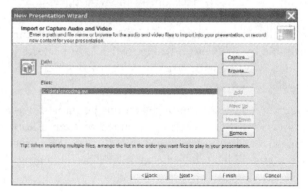

Figure 10.3.
Importing audio and video.

Click the Capture button to capture video from within Producer, which is the only way to prevent Producer from re-encoding your video during final rendering. For example, if you edit your video in another program and output a Windows Media file into Producer, the program will re-encode the video during final rendering even if it matches the target resolution and bitrate perfectly.

Since double compression always degrades quality, it's best to capture within Producer if you can. Fortunately, Producer offers simple splitting and trimming controls that allow you to edit your video to a certain degree, as well as transitions and effects. But if you need to insert titles, you're out of luck.

If you have to produce your video in a third-party editor, you have two choices. First, you can output the finished file back to your DV camera and capture anew from inside Producer. Alternatively, you can output a high-bitrate Windows Media file from your video editor, which will minimize the degradation caused by the double compression. If you choose this route, make sure you output at the resolution used by your template; otherwise Producer will have to scale the video as well as recompress it.

Capturing

Click the capture button in the Import or Capture Audio and Video dialog to open Producer's capture wizard. Most screens are straightforward, so I won't detail them here.

To avoid double compression of the captured file during final rendering, you must make sure the captured file matches the ultimate target output parameters. For this you have to meet three requirements:

- You must capture using the Target audience you intend to select during rendering (in this case Corporate LAN connection at 300Kbps, as shown in **Figure 10.4**).

- You must capture at the resolution used by your template (in this case, 320x240).

- You must capture using the codec you plan to use during publishing (in this case, Windows Media 9).

Unless all three conditions are met, Producer will re-encode the file during final production.

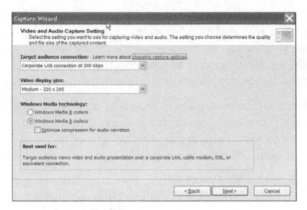

Figure 10.4.
Make sure capture parameters match your target output.

Synchronizing Your Content

If you've imported slides, the next dialog will ask if you'd like to synchronize their appearance to the audio and/or video. Answer Yes; otherwise Producer will simply assign default time values to the slides and build the presentation.

Click Next and then Finish and Producer starts loading your content into the program. If you clicked Yes in the Synchronize Presentation dialog shown in **Figure 10.5**, Producer will display the screen shown in **Figure 10.6** after loading all selected content into the program. This is how you'll synchronize your slides to the inserted audio or video.

Operation is simple. Use the player controls shown in Figure 10.6 to move to each point in the audio or video file where you want the new slide to appear. Typically, I play the video in real time to hear the verbal cues, then pause the video and use the previous frame or next frame controls to back up or move forwards as necessary.

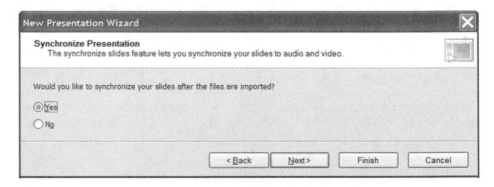

Figure 10.5. Click Yes here to synchronize slides with audio and/or video.

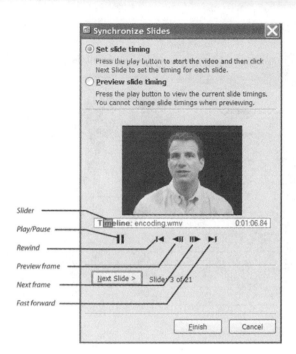

Slider

Play/Pause

Rewind

Preview frame

Next frame

Fast forward

Figure 10.6.
Synchronizing slide appearance
to the video file.

Then click the Next Slide button, and move to the next insertion point. The controls provide frame-accurate positioning, so you should be able to position the appearance of the new slide when the speaker first refers to it. Take the time to get the positioning right at this stage, because changing synchronization later is not as efficient.

Working in the Producer Timeline

Click Finish, and Producer opens the main Producer interface, shown in **Figure 10.7**. The program has a basic four-window interface, with a Windows Explorer file manager on the left (Tree pane), a library window in the top center for selecting content (Contents pane), transitions and effects, a preview window on the upper right (Monitor), and a timeline on the bottom.

Take a look at the different tracks on the timeline. As you can see, the Video and Audio tracks contain the respective tracks from the imported video file, with the Transition track available when the video timeline contains multiple clips. The Slide track contains the PowerPoint slides; alternatively, you can insert digital pictures here to create a simple slideshow.

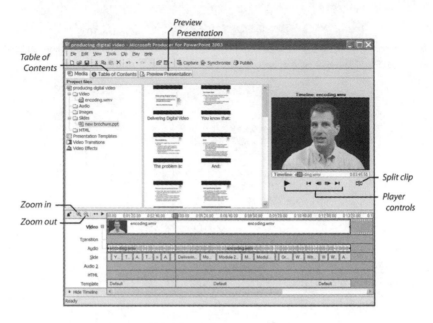

Figure 10.7. Producer's main interface.

You can add another audio track to Audio 2. To adjust the relative volume of the two tracks, choose Tools > Audio Levels. The HTML track can contain Web pages to display in the presentation, or Web links; this is discussed below in Inserting Web Links. Finally, the template track contains the template chosen at the first stage of producing this presentation.

A few points about working in Producer's timeline:

- First, as in most timelines, you can zoom in to set details, and zoom back out for the big picture. Use the two magnifying lenses located on the left, just above the video track, to zoom in and out.

- Second, locate the Split video button just beneath the video window on the right. To edit content from an audio or video file, use the player controls beneath the video window to move to the desired split point. Then, click the split button, and trim away unwanted video by dragging the edge to the desired frame, as shown in **Figure 10.8**. Producer automatically closes any gap you create to prevent gaps in the presentation.

- Third, you can drag any asset on the timeline by simply grabbing it with your cursor and dragging it to the target location. I'm making this sound way too hard; if you're at all familiar with video editors, you'll find Producer's timeline a snap to use.

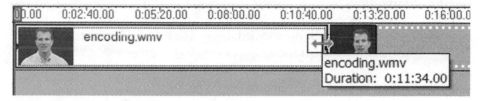

Figure 10.8. After splitting the clip, drag the edge to the desired frame.

Polishing Your Text

During the production process, Producer uses the titles from your PowerPoint slides to create the list shown beneath the player window in Figure 10.1. However, sometimes these titles provide little guidance regarding the contents of the slide. For this reason, Producer allows you to change the title text and also organize your titles into sections for enhanced interactivity.

For example, in **Figure 10.9**—accessed by clicking the Table of Contents button on the upper left of the main screen (see Figure 10.7)—you can see the titles as originally imported from PowerPoint. The fourth title simply says "And:," which tells the viewer nothing about the content of the slide. To change this, click Change in the middle of the screen, which opens the Table of Contents Entry window shown on the bottom right of Figure 10.9. Don't change the selected value in the Associate with: list box; use the existing value.

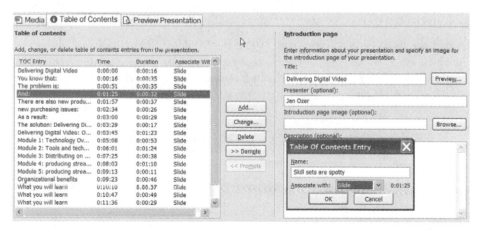

Figure 10.9. Use this screen to organize your presentation.

Use the Demote and Promote buttons to organize your content. Demote moves your text 15 pixels to the right, while Promote moves your text 15 pixels to the left. When you're done, click the Media tab to return to the main screen, or the Preview Presentation tab to preview.

Inserting Web Links

Before I preview, however, there's one piece of content to add—a link to the Web page containing the course brochure and signup information. It would be a pretty sorry sales video without a specific call to action.

First, a few preliminary points. I'm adding an HTML screen near the end of the presentation, and don't want it to appear *during* the presentation. However, all content added to the timeline snaps back to the beginning of the timeline to prevent content gaps (even if you *intended* to have gaps). So even if I insert it at Minute 14, the HTML page will snap back to the start of the timeline.

To work around this default, I used a template that displays PowerPoint slides (not HTML) during the main presentation, then switched to a template that displayed HTML (not PowerPoint slides) when I wanted the HTML page to appear. Fortunately, Microsoft includes templates with these combinations in the same video window. Though it sounds complicated, it's simple once you know what you have to do, and pretty easy to set up.

To switch templates, click Presentation Templates in the Tree pane to display all templates in the Contents pane. Drag the new template down to the Template track in the timeline, and drag the edges so it's positioned correctly.

To add the link, choose File > Add Web Link, which opens the dialog shown in **Figure 10.10**. You can display the Web page within the presentation by checking Display live page, or display only the link by clicking that option. Then, Producer will activate the Text field so you can type a description.

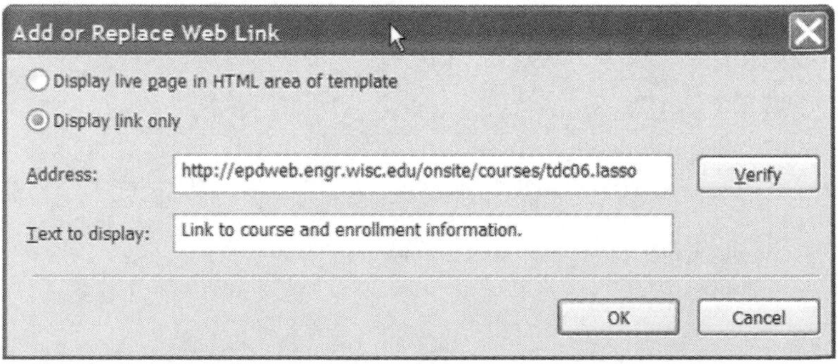

Figure 10.10. Adding a Web link to the presentation.

After you press OK, Producer adds the new link to the HTML folder. Click HTML in the Tree pane, and you should see the new link in the Contents pane. Drag it down to the HTML track to add it to the project.

Preview and Adjust Synchronization

At this point, you're ready to preview, so click the Preview Presentation tab shown on the top of Figure 10.9. If you have lots of titles, many will likely be obscured by the timeline. To close the timeline for complete preview, select View > Timeline, or click Ctrl+T on your keyboard.

When you preview, your primary concern is synchronizing the slides with the audio, so click each title and make sure it appears about the time the speaker first refers to it. To adjust the synchronization of a slide, click the Media tab to return to the timeline.

Follow these steps to the fastest way to adjust your synchronization, as shown in **Figure 10.11:**

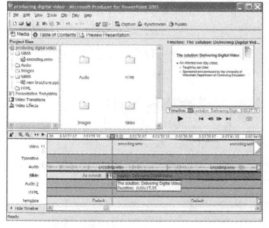

Figure 10.11.
Adjusting synchronization in the timeline.

- Click the video track to display the video in the upper right preview window.

- Use the player controls to move to the point in the video where you want the slide to appear. This will also move the edit line on the timeline to the new target position.

- Click and activate the slide track.

- Hover your cursor over the edges of the slides you need to adjust, and when the drag cursor appears, drag the edge to the edit line, which Producer will automatically snap to. Producer will adjust the edges of the two slides as necessary, without changing their total duration so your adjustment doesn't change the synchronization of subsequent slides.

Publishing Your Presentation

After polishing and previewing, it's time to publish. Start by clicking the Publish button in the Producer toolbar, which opens the screen shown in **Figure 10.12**.

It's simple to publish onto your hard disk (for potentially transferring to CD) or to any place on your network where you have sharing rights. If you want to write directly to a Web server, it must be a Windows Media Services streaming server, either hosted by your organization, or by a third party. If you click Web Server in the Publish Wizard, a "Learn More" button appears which you can click to see a list of Producer-compatible service providers.

You can also post your presentation to Microsoft's SharePoint Services Web site or SharePoint Portal Server. For details on all these Web-based uploads, see the Microsoft white paper located here:

www.microsoft.com/downloads/details.aspx?FamilyId=AFC52625-E1B6-4A1A-9EEB-106C878713CB&displaylang=en.

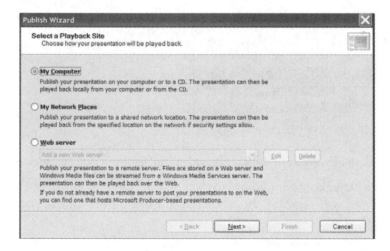

Figure 10.12. Producer's Publish Wizard.

Choosing Encoding Parameters

After choosing your playback site, you'll page through a screen for posting information about the presentation and then a Publish Settings screen where you'll choose your encoding parameters. The default setting is optimized for your content, and will vary from project to project. If it's acceptable, click Next, otherwise check Choose Publish Settings for Additional Audiences, and then click Next to open the window shown in **Figure 10.13**. Here you have a number of options that require explaining.

In the Windows Media Technology dropdown box, you can select Windows Media 9 codecs, Windows Media 8 codecs, or both. Use Windows Media 8 if you're concerned about playback compatibility with older computers, Windows Media 9 if your audience is exclusively Windows 98 SE and above on the Windows side, and OS X on the Mac, or you can choose both; in this case Producer will create different files for both codecs.

Check the Enable Rich-Media Streaming checkbox if you're streaming from a Windows Media Streaming server, and Producer will customize the encoded files automatically. If your audio is speech-only, check Optimize Compression for Audio Narration, and Producer will use a codec optimized for voice.

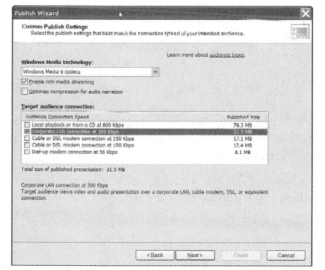

Figure 10.13.
Here's where you define your target audience and check other encoding parameters.

If you choose multiple target audiences, Producer will output multiple files and provide a viewer with different bitrate alternatives. Click Next and Producer displays the encoding progress screen (**Figure 10.14**) but won't actually begin encoding until you click Next again.

Once the presentation is published, Producer will allow you to preview how the file will look in three different browsers: Internet Explorer 5.0 for Windows, Internet Explorer 5.2.2 (or later) for Mac OS X, and Netscape Navigator 7.0 for Windows. I saw some minor differences, and suggest you test thoroughly if you're distributing to Macintosh and Netscape clients.

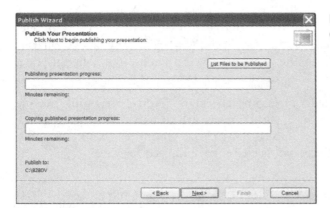

Figure 10.14.
Click Next to start encoding.

Final Tips

We've covered a fair amount of Producer's capabilities, but there are a couple of additional functions you should know about. First, as a default, Microsoft displays a link to the Producer Web page on its Web site in all presentations. You can eliminate this by selecting Tools > Options and then uncheck the Display a Web Link on the Introduction Page checkbox.

Once you're in the Options window, click the Timeline tab and adjust default durations if desired. I found the defaults too long for my liking.

Finally, to get a good feel for the capabilities of Producer, check out the samples on Microsoft's Producer Web site here:

www.microsoft.com/office/powerpoint/producer/prodinfo/default.mspx.

Chapter 11:
Producing and Deploying Closed Captions

Whether you work in a government facility, in academia, or for a contractor supplying video to the government, your work must meet the accessibility standards of Section 508 of the Rehabilitation Act of 1973 (see *www.section508.gov*). As one regulation states, "All training and informational video and multimedia productions which support the agency's mission, regardless of format, that contain speech or other audio information necessary for the comprehension of the content, shall be open or closed captioned." That's a big net that catches a lot of government and academic videos.

This chapter starts with a look at closed-captioning issues such as what to caption, and how closed captions differ from DVD subtitles. Once you decide to caption, your next step is to set captioning standards to ensure consistency within and among your video productions. The following section will examine the most important issues to consider when establishing your captioning standards.

Then I'll describe the captioning workflow, starting with how to format your files for import into a captioning program. Using a remarkable program called MAGpie, we'll synchronize a set of sample captions to a video file and integrate the results with Windows Media, RealVideo, and QuickTime videos.

If you're producing both streaming videos and DVDs, you'll need to produce one text stream to work with both formats. As a final step, I'll identify the tools and suggest a workflow for doing just that.

Before going further, let me acknowledge the kind assistance from two captioning professionals who helped shape this chapter. First, thanks to Cynthia M. King, Ph.D, executive director, academic technology at Gallaudet University, for providing access to her staff and a thorough "tech read" of the chapter. Also, Andrew Kirkpatrick from the Media Access Group at WGBH in Boston provided invaluable insight into the inner workings of MAGpie2, the captioning tool from the Media Access Group, and how closed captions are implemented by Apple,

Microsoft, and Real in their respective formats. I also appreciate Andrew's careful "tech read" of this chapter.

Preliminary Issues

Note that closed captions play a broader role than the subtitles you may have seen in foreign movies or DVDs. That's because most subtitles assume that the viewer can *hear*, but doesn't understand the language. For this reason, noises such as gunshots, screams, music welling up, dogs barking, and cars beeping may not be noted in the subtitle text.

Closed captions assume that the viewer *cannot* hear. For that reason, to comply with Section 508, closed captions must "contain speech or other audio information necessary for the comprehension of the content." If you're producing a DVD for government use, you'll need to add all the audio cues necessary to satisfy this requirement.

It's important to note that captioning for broadcast and captioning for streaming video and DVD involve completely different techniques and technologies. Captioning for broadcast involves expensive hardware and software to insert the captioned text directly into the video file.

In contrast, captioning for streaming and DVD involves creating text files in inexpensive (or free) shareware programs and then linking the text file to the video file for streaming, or importing the text file into the DVD authoring program to create subtitles. While some broadcast captioning systems can export text strings for DVD and streaming, if you're not concerned with broadcast, inexpensive programs function just as well.

This chapter focuses entirely on closed captioning for streaming video and DVD and does not address broadcast-specific requirements or technologies. It also focuses solely on the captioning requirements for on-demand files; live event captioning uses a different set of rules and obviously different transcription requirements.

Creating Your Captioning Standard

There are few absolute right or wrong precedents in captioning; what's most important is to be consistent in how captions are created and applied. Before creating your first closed-captioned text, you should define the conventions you'll use to produce your closed captions. I'll cover a list of decisions to consider when creating your captioning standards, along with some suggested approaches.

194

In formulating these standards, I relied heavily on the standards and practices used by the Media Access Group at WGBH in Boston, the world's first captioning agency. The people there have been delivering accessible media to disabled adults, students, and their families, teachers, and friends for more than 30 years. Certain areas I address are largely paraphrased from materials from the Media Access Group, with the group's gracious permission. You can find the Media Access Group's excellent captioning the guide at *http://main.wgbh.org/wgbh/pages/mag/services/captioning/faq/sugg-styles-conv-faq.html#copy*.

The most detailed captioning guide I found (with help from Judy Harkins at Gallaudet University's Technology Access Program) was produced by the Captioned Media Program (CMP) of the National Association of the Deaf, which can be found at *www.cfv.org/caai/nadh7.pdf.* If you're looking for one document that contains highly detailed recommendations for nearly all caption-related questions (and why wouldn't you?), this is it.

The CMP's style guide incorporates consumer research performed by the Technology Access Program at Gallaudet University and summarized at *tap.gallaudet.edu/nsi_recom.htm.* This link contains a great document for understanding the philosophy behind the CMP practices and procedures. Another resource addressing a variety of captioning issues, including closed captioning tools, is Gary Robson's FAQ, found at *www.robson.org/capfaq.*

For a general perspective on the practices followed by several captioning services, check out Joe Clark's article in *Print* magazine, "Typography and TV Captioning." Though originally published in 1989, it's still a great (and relevant) read, and can still find it online at: *www.joeclark.org/design/print/print1989.html,* and other valuable material from Joe at *www.joeclark.org/access/captioning.*

Step 1: How Many Lines

The first decision you'll make in defining your captioning standard is how many lines of captions. Television captions tend to be three or four lines, while most Hollywood DVD titles tend to use two lines.

Most streaming producers also use two lines. Some companies, such as the Media Access Group, add a third line at the top of the caption to identify the speaker (**Figure 11.1**). Unless you have a strong reason to choose otherwise, two lines of text is probably a good place to start. More on the speaker identification issue later.

Figure 11.1.
Two lines of text plus a separate line to identify the speaker.

Step 2: Which Captioning Technique?

There are three styles used to make captions appear and disappear from the screen:

- *Roll-up captions*—These captions scroll up like credits at the end of a movie, line by line, and remain onscreen until pushed out of the viewing area. In a three-line caption, the first line remains onscreen until the fourth line appears to push it off screen.

- *Paint-on captions*—This technique literally paints the captions onscreen from left to right. Each letter is filled in individually and sequentially, one line after another, until the caption area is fully painted on. The caption area then goes blank for a moment and the next caption begins painting again. Note that paint-on captions are available only for TV, not for streaming media or DVD.

- *Pop-on captions*—These captions appear all at once and remain onscreen until removed (at which point the caption area goes blank) or is replaced by the next caption.

Paint-on appears to be the preferred approach for movies and other nonlive media, and is the only approach sanctioned by the Captioned Media Program. If you choose Roll-up captions, most of the rules identified next apply, except that two "greater than" symbols should appear before each new speaker.

For example, the text in Figure 11.1 would appear as follows:

```
>> KEN: Joining us here

is Mr. Jan Ozer.
```

Sometimes in newscasts, three "greater than" symbols are used to indicate a change from one story to another.

Step 3: Tips on Text Segmentation

Let's step back for a minute and consider what's actually happening when you convert a script or transcribed speech into captions. Most conversations involve a give and take between two or more individuals. Sometimes a comment from one might be a single word like "yes" or "no." Sometimes a response can be three or four sentences long, involving dozens of words.

Irrespective of the length of the speaker's comments, during captioning we break them down into their most comprehensible chunks. One very relevant chunk is the number of lines within a caption. If you choose two-line captions, this means that all dialog must be subdivided into chunks of two lines each.

However, each line must also be limited to a certain number of characters for optimum readability. For example, the Captioned Media Program requires a maximum of 32 characters per line—a hard limit due to the limitations in television displays. While streaming and DVD formats have more flexibility, you should try to average between 30 and 35 characters per line, *including spaces*.

So to recap, you must subdivide all speech into two-line chunks, each containing approximately 30 to 35 characters per line. It doesn't matter if you're captioning Rhett Butler's famous last words in *Gone With the Wind* ("Frankly, my dear...") or the Presidential State of the Union address; you've got to break it down in the same way.

At a high level, when dividing up your text, understand that people don't read letter by letter or even word by word, they read in chunks of words, or phrases. For this reason, captions are most readable when divided into logical phrases, both *within* the two lines in a caption and *from caption to caption*. I've illustrated this in **Table 11.1**.

Table 11.1. Breaking captions into logical phrases.

	Good Logical Phrasing	Poor Logical Phrasing
Caption 1:	Joining us here is Mr. Jan Ozer,	Joining us here is Mr. Jan Ozer, a contributing
Caption 2:	a contributing editor for New York's PC Magazine.	editor for New York's PC Magazine. Welcome Jan.
Caption 3:	Welcome Jan.	

The phrasing on the right violates both rules; there's poor phrasing *within* Caption 1 (breaking up a name) and *between* Captions 1 and 2 (breaking up a title). If you read both versions out loud, you'll instantly see that the first column reads much more naturally. "If it sounds like good phrasing, it probably is good phrasing" is the general approach, but for some truly definitive rules, go to page 10 of the Captioned Media Program document I referenced earlier.

Column 2 (right) violates another rule of segmentation: a period should always end a caption (though not all captions have to end with periods). Specifically, in Caption 2, where the first sentence ends with "Magazine," the next sentence should start a new caption, as it does on the left.

Here's what we've learned from this section (with one additional point):

- Segment multiple lines within a caption into logical phrases.

- Segment multiple lines of captions into logical phrases.

- The end of a sentence ends a caption line.

- Start a new caption each time the speaker changes.

Now that you have your text divided into captions, it's time to decide how to present the text.

Step 4: Choose Your Font and Case

Typically, when it comes to print or static (onscreen) text, fonts with serifs, such as Times New Roman, are more readable than sans serif fonts, and words are more recognizable, since most books and magazines use fonts with serifs. The Media Access Group recommends using the Roman font, and Times New Roman is the most similar font installed on most computers.

However, some research indicates that sans serif fonts work better for closed captions than fonts with a serif (there's more information on this at *www.joeclark.org/access/captioning/bpoc/typography.html*). According to Gallaudet officials, in their experience sans serif fonts are more readable. The Captioned Media Program appears to share this view, as it chose Helvetica Medium, a sans serif font, as its standard. All in all then, sans serif fonts are probably the best choice.

As discussed in Chapter 5, text with mixed capitals and lowercase lettering is easier to read than all uppercase text, and therefore the recommended practice for streaming media and DVDs. If you think that recommendation differs from most television captions, you're correct, and here's why.

Most closed-caption decoders on TV sets can't display the below-the-line segments of letters such as j, g, q, and y (also called descenders). Instead, they display the entire letter above the line, producing a distracting appearance that decreases legibility. That's why television uses all caps. Streaming technologies and DVDs don't have these limitations, so you're free to use the more readable mixed-case lettering.

Step 5: Choose Your Font Size

Font sizes vary by captioning program, making it impossible to recommend a specific font size. In general, larger fonts are obviously more readable, but if your font is too large, your caption will wrap to the next line, or extend outside the viewing area.

There are also stylistic elements to consider. For example, PBS programs tend to use very small but elegant captions that torture my 40-something eyes (for example, see *www.pbs.org/wgbh/nova/*). Those shown on the Web site of the National Center for Accessible Media (part of the Media Access Group) are much larger and much more readable (see, for example, *http://ncam.wgbh.org/richmedia/examples/92.html*).

My recommendation is to prioritize readability over elegance. In deciding what font size to use, preview your options within your target player. MAGpie was a fantastic tool, but the appearance of the font size within its preview window didn't always accurately represent what ultimately appeared in the player.

Step 6: Define Text Placement and Speaker Identification

Here we'll discuss where to place your captions within (or underneath) the screen, and how and when you announce your speaker. As you would suspect, placement of text, in certain situations, can provide strong clues as to who is speaking. For this reason, in Figure 11.1, the text is positioned on the right, underneath the interviewer, Ken Santucci.

This leads us to Rule Number One in caption placement; if there are two consistently placed speakers, place captions beneath their respective positions. Note that under television rules, both captions, irrespective of placement, would be left-justified. However, since many streaming formats can't display left-justified text on the right side of the screen, you should right-justify text placed on the right, and left-justify text placed on the left.

If there's only one speaker, place the caption in the center of the screen and center-justify the text. In addition, if the speaker is *off-screen*, include the name or identification of the speaker, place the caption in the screen center and center-justify the text.

You should also identify the speaker whenever the viewer has no clear visual clues as to their identity. For example, if the video starts up and an off-screen narrator begins to speak, you should identify the speaker as narrator. If your interview has a J-cut, where the audio from the second video starts playing while the first video remains onscreen (see Chapter 5), you should identify the speaker.

If there are multiple on-screen speakers in a fast-paced discussion, consider identifying the speaker in all captions. Alternatively, since most speakers talk for longer than one or two captions, consider identifying the speaker only when the speaker changes.

As speaker identification is not spoken information, typically it's set off from the main captioning in some way. For example, in Figure 11.1, the speaker identification is positioned on its own line, in all caps, placed in brackets, and set off with a colon, which is the practice of the Media Access Group. The Captioned Media Program uses italics or brackets, with no colon, and also positions the title on its own line.

In contrast, PBS, in its closed-captioned streaming videos, uses all caps offset with a colon, on the same line as the first line in the caption, which looks like this:

```
KEN: Joining us here

is Mr. Jan Ozer.
```

Gallaudet's recommendation is prescient in this regard. "If the character cannot be identified by name, then a descriptor should be provided," he states. "An acceptable format for explicit identification is the character's name or descriptor in upper/lower case, surrounded by parentheses, above the caption and left-justified with the caption. Other formats are probably uncontroversial." Basically, pick one approach, and apply it consistently.

Let's break these rules down for easy scanning:

- *If there are two consistently positioned speakers*—Place captions on their respective sides of the screen, justifying to their respective sides.

- *If there is only one speaker*—Place captions in the center of the screen and center-justify them.

- *If the speaker is offscreen*—Place captions in the center of the screen and center-justify them. Some producers identify off-screen speakers with italics.

- *Clearly identify new speakers whenever speaker identification is not obvious to the viewer*—This can occur with off-screen narration, during J-cuts, or when there are many speakers on screen. Format your speaker identification to distinguish it from spoken text.

There's one real-world caveat to these rules: not all players and/or closed-captioned tools can create or implement left-justified, right-justified, and centered captions. For example, because of alignment problems encountered when playing closed-captioned streams in Windows Media Player, the Media Access Group modified MAGpie to produce only left-placed captions. In addition, RealPlayer can only display left and center-aligned captions (though, of course, you could right-justify the text using space or tab commands). In fact, the only streaming player that properly implemented our speaker-placement strategy was QuickTime.

Positioning within a DVD stream was a little more straightforward, and should be feasible in most authoring programs. Still, before selecting a caption-positioning strategy, test to ensure that all development tools and/or players comply with the strategy.

Step 7: Define Rules for Noises and Other Points of Emphasis

As we've discussed already, closed captions must describe a broad range of audio events to enhance the viewer's comprehension of the video. As with speaker identifications, these audio events need to be visually different from the spoken information.

The Media Access Group recommends showing sound-effect captions parenthetically, in lowercase italics (but don't italicize the parentheses), typically presented as a standalone caption. In the context of our interview footage, which was shot during the hustle and bustle of a trade show, captions included the one shown in **Figure 11.2**, displayed as the video is fading in from black at the start. This lets the viewer know that we're shooting in a crowd, and you should identify both the source of the noise and the noise itself.

Figure 11.2. Captioning audio events.

You can use these same indicators to describe the intonations that flavor the speech. In the interview, Ken and I were swapping stories, and he recalled a joint presentation where the equipment setup went less than smoothly. I laughed, and commented, "What a mess that was!" This would be captioned as shown in **Figure 11.3**. It's also appropriate to caption emotion (e.g., angry frown, deep in thought, daydreaming) even if there is no accompanying speech.

(*laughing*)
What a mess that was!

Figure 11.3. Captioning the speaker's intonation.

The styles shown in Figures 11.2 and 11.3 are from the Media Access Group. The Captioned Media Program recommends brackets instead of parenthesis, and places on-screen noises and intonations in normal case, and off-screen noises in italics.

It's acceptable to use onomatopoeia, or text strings that sound like the noise being described, though Gallaudet University found that most consumers preferred both a text description and onomatopoeia.

These would appear as follows:

```
(dog growling)
Grrrrrrr,
```

or

```
(putt drops into cup)
Kerplunk!
```

In addition to noises and sound effects, consider identifying other information that's apparent in the audio but not in the text description. This would include accents (e.g., French accent), audience reaction (laughing, loud boos) and the pace of speech (slow drawl).

Step 8: Choose Your Music Treatment

Music often sets the mood of the video, so when background music is present, it should be indicated. Television sets use a special musical note character to identify music playing, or when someone is singing, but the character is not universally recognized by all streaming media players. If it's not available to you, use the word music in italics surrounded by either parenthesis (Media Access Group) or brackets (Captioned Media Program).

If the music has no lyrics, be as descriptive as possible (soothing music, disco music) and identify the name and the composer if known. Caption the lyrics if they are being sung, starting and ending with the special music character.

Step 9: Editing the Text

The goal with captions is to present them with the actual spoken word, but some people talk faster than others can read. In these instances, it's accepted practice to edit the text to achieve a certain reading speed.

In this regard, the Captioned Media Program guide presents some very interesting statistics about reading rates along with very clear guidelines. Specifically, the guide states that most elementary or secondary students can read at 120 words per minute (wpm), and adults up to 160 wpm. For Captioned Media Program videos, the guide requires that "no caption should remain onscreen less than 2 seconds or exceed 235 wpm."

When editing the text, the Media Access Group advises that caption producers "try to maintain precisely the original meaning and flavor of the language as well as the personality of the speaker. Avoid editing only a single word from a sentence as this doesn't really extend reading time. Similarly, avoid substituting one longer word for two shorter words (even write a shorter word for a longer word) or simply making a contraction from two words (e.g., contracting 'should not' to 'shouldn't')."

Note that virtually all style guides recommend *against* modifying for correct English (substituting "isn't" for "ain't," or "you all" for "y'all"). Finally, if you find yourself having to shorten major sections of speech to meet your desired wpm rate, page 14 of the Captioned Media Program style guide offers some great guidelines.

Step 10: Other Issues

The first nine steps covered the main issues, but there are many additional standards to address. Two of the most common include:

*   *Treatment of numbers*—Generally spell out one through ten, numerals for higher numbers except when they start a sentence (Media Access Group).

*   *Acronyms*—Display as normal (IEEE rather then eye-triple e)

For others, such as fractions, dates, dollar amounts, and more, consult the Captioned Media Program style guide.

Creating Your Closed-Captioned Text

You have your style guide; now you're ready to begin formatting your text. The first step is to convert the audio into a text file. You can tackle this problem in a number of ways.

Manual Conversion

First let's deal with manual conversion. Here a transcriber listens to the audio and enters all speech and other audio information into a file in a word processor. Then the transcriber starts breaking the file into individual captions according to standards used by the closed-captioning program. For example, MAGpie has very specific requirements for text input.

Manual conversion can be very time-consuming. Some sources estimate that television programs and movies rich in nonspeech audio content such as sound effects, background music, and drama, can take up to 20 hours of conversion for each hour of audio. Most corporate or academic training materials should be much shorter, since most of the text is simply transcribed speech. If you have a script that was largely followed, this provides a good starting point.

A quick Google search under "closed captioning services" revealed a number of service bureaus with prices starting at the $6 per minute range, or less than $200 for a 30-minute production. While certainly not cheap, this is a fraction of most production costs, especially if you had to rent equipment, a soundstage, or pay actors or other related personnel.

If you go the service bureau route, when obtaining a quote, be sure to ask the following questions:

- What digital and analog captioning formats does the bureau support (Windows Media, QuickTime, Real, Line 21, DVD)?
- What level of accuracy will the service bureau guarantee?
- What style of captions will the service bureau produce (roll-up, paint-on, pop-on)?
- How will the service bureau segment the text (characters per line and lines per caption)?
- Will charges include complete audio transcription (sound effects, intonations) or just speech?
- Which style guide or other direction will the service bureau use to segment the text and caption information, such as dates, numbers, and the like?

Speech Recognition

Automatic speech recognition generally works best when tuned to the voice and speech pattern of one user. For this reason, plugging in the audio feed from a training video or lecture involving random individuals will almost always produce poor-quality results.

To avoid this problem, many universities (including Gallaudet's Television and Media Production Service) have adopted "shadowing" or "voice writing" where a person trained on the software repeats every word spoken in the video into the voice recognition system. Typically, these individuals work in a quiet environment or use a mask to minimize outside interference. These systems are not 100 percent accurate, but they do provide a first draft that can accelerate the transcriber's work.

Computer Prompting and Captioning Company (CPC), a prominent closed captioned vendor, sells several systems that include IBM ViaVoice speech recognition software (*www.cpcweb.com/Captioning/cap_via_voice.htm*). You can also read about Gallaudet's experience with shadowing here:

http://tap.gallaudet.edu/SpeechRecog.htm.

Converting Broadcast Closed Captions

Most current television programs include closed captioning, which you can capture and reformat for use in streaming content. Grabbing the closed-captioned text itself can be fairly inexpensive, as most All-In-Wonder products from ATI have offered this feature for years (*www.ati.com/products/radeon8500/ aiwradeon8500/ faq.html*). Of course, from there, you have to reformat the text as necessary for your ultimate use.

To streamline this process, in fall 2004, The Media Access Group's research arm, NCAM (National Center for Accessible Media), announced CaptionKeeper, which captures broadcast captions (also called Line 21 captions) and converts them to Real or Windows Media captions ready for live streaming or archiving.

The fee to license CaptionKeeper is $1,000 for corporations and $500 for academic institutions. Third-party hardware is required to capture the Line 21 captions, which will probably add about $800 to the entire system price. Check NCAM's Web site for more details (*http://ncam.wgbh.org/*). Note that while the Media Access Group promised to provide details about these products on its Web site, there was nothing posted at press time.

Converting Your Text to Closed Captions

Once you have a transcription of your audio, your work has just begun. Typically, your transcription will list each speaker and their comments in paragraph style, and may or may not have background noises, speech inflections, or other additions necessary to provide complete comprehension of the event.

As a starting point, your transcription may look like this:

```
Ken: We're streaming today live with both the Real encoder and
the Microsoft Windows encoder, side by side.

Jan: Very politically correct.

Ken: That's another interesting thing. There's more and more of
the streaming codecs available, especially at this show. We just
talked with Apple about QuickTime, and there are several new
ones. We'll talk to those authors, tomorrow.
```

Now the task is to add the required sound effects and format the text as specified in your style sheet. You should also look at the requirements of your captioning software. For example, MAGpie assumes that a single carriage return separates two lines within a single caption, while a double carriage return means a new caption.

If I input the text as shown in the sample transcript, MAGpie would produce three two-line captions, but the first and third would contain far too many characters. To avoid this, and remove the names (I'll show who's speaking by positioning the captions), I would pre-format the file as follows:

```
We're streaming today live with both the Real encoder and the
Microsoft Windows encoder, side by side.

Very politically correct.

That's another interesting thing. (both laugh)

There's more and more of the streaming codecs available, espe-
cially at this show.

We just talked with Apple about QuickTime, and there are sev-
eral new ones.

We'll talk to those authors, tomorrow.
```

I also added the "(*both laugh*)" caption to reflect that both Ken and I were laughing after the "politically correct" quip. As we'll see, preformatting the file in this manner importing into MAGpie a snap. If you decide to try MAGpie, be sure to check out NCAM's page on preformatting documents for MAGpie *http://ncam.wgbh.org/richmedia/tutorials/transcriptpreformat.html.*

If you decide to use another captioning program, check the manual for preformatting tips for that product. Bear in mind, most captioning programs won't accept Word for Windows .DOC files, so save the file as a plain text file with a .TXT extension.

Creating Closed Captions with MAGpie

If you're using a broadcast captioning system, you should first ask your vendor if the system can generate captions in your target format—either QuickTime, Windows Media, or Real.

You can find a relatively complete list of captioning tools at *www.captions.org/softlinks.cfm*. MAGpie, developed by NCAM, is one of the most popular tools, and downloaded for free at *http://ncam.wgbh.org/webaccess/magpie/*.

On the download page, you'll see that installing MAGpie involves several elements, including the Java Virtual Machine, which actually runs the program. Print and follow these installation instructions carefully, otherwise the program won't run—I know because I didn't, and it didn't. One uninstall and meticulous reinstall later, and everything was fine.

MAGpie works most efficiently when applying captions to the actual compressed file you'll be distributing, so if you haven't encoded your file, do so before starting. With this and your captions file properly formatted, you're ready to start.

MAGpie's interface has two windows, one to play the video and the other to format the captions and synchronize them to the video stream. Since all controls are on the synchronization screen, I'll mostly show shots of that screen, though if you jump ahead to Figure 11.10, you can see the Player.

Open MAGpie, then click File > New Project in MAGpie's file menu. MAGpie's Open New Project screen appears (**Figure 11.4**). You can return to this screen at any time by clicking File > Properties.

Click the Browse button on the top right to load your media file. Then click the radio button if you're captioning a QuickTime file, or the Oratrix GRiNS Player if you're captioning a Windows Media or Real Video file. I'm working with a Windows Media file, so I'll choose the GRiNS player.

As you can see, MAGpie allows you to set separate text options for the Caption and Speaker identification styles. Interestingly, though the Media Access Group's default font is Roman, the default for this tool is Arial, with a white font against a black background. To save a trip back later, click each style and boost the font size to 18, which is what we'll use in our final captions. Accept all other font defaults.

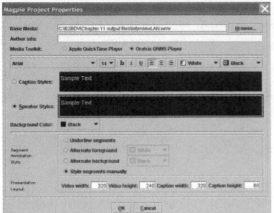

Figure 11.4.
MAGpie's Project Properties screen.

The Segment Annotation style is an advanced feature that applies Karaoke-style labeling to the captions. Leave this at the default setting (Style segments manually). If your video file is not 320x240, adjust the video parameters to those of your file, and adjust caption width and height accordingly. For example, if your file is 640x480, enter that into the video width and height fields, and make the caption width 640, and the caption height 480. Then, click OK.

Next, MAGpie displays the Create New Project Track screen (**Figure 11.5**) where you choose the type and name of the track. Audio descriptions are audio files containing narrated descriptions of the video for those with impaired vision, which is an entirely different operation, which I'll cover later in this chapter. Make sure Captions are clicked, and either accept the track name (as I've done) or enter a new one, and click OK.

Figure 11.5.
This screen chooses between captions and audio descriptions.

After you click this screen, the main MAGpie interface should appear with your video in a separate player. Now let's insert the text file containing the captions. Right click on Track One, and choose Insert Captions from File (**Figure 11.6**).

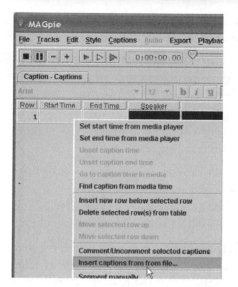

Figure 11.6.
Right-click and choose Insert Captions from File.

MAGpie opens a standard File Open dialog, which you should use to select and load your file. Note that MAGpie loads your file starting on Row 2 of the captions. It's not necessary, but if you'd like to delete Row 1 so your captions start on Row 1, just click the blank line, right click, and choose Delete Selected Row. When you're done, MAGpie should look like it does in **Figure 11.7**.

As you can see, each caption row has a column for Start and End time. You don't have to insert an End time; if that column is blank, MAGpie simply replaces the caption with the subsequent caption at its designated start time. The only reason to insert an End time is if you'd like the closed-captioned screen area to go blank.

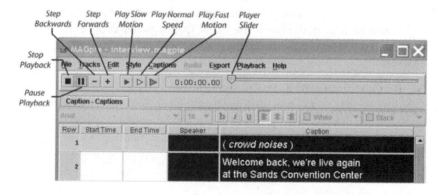

Figure 11.7. Use MAGpie's player controls to search around the file.

Note the player controls on the top of the MAGpie menu. Use these to play the file in the player, which should be located in a separate window on the left. Alternatively, you can press F6 to start and stop the video.

Synchronizing Captions and Audio

To start synchronizing captions to audio, click Row 1 and make sure you're at the absolute start of the video file. Click F9, and MAGpie will insert 0:00:00.00 to synchronize the video starting point with the first row.

MAGpie then automatically advances to the next caption row. Use the player controls to advance the video to where the next caption should appear and press F9 again. With a little practice, you should be able to play the video in real time, and press the F9 key to synchronize each row with the associated audio.

It forces you to concentrate, but I focus on the penultimate word in each caption. When I hear that word, I press F9, and read ahead and find the penultimate word of the next caption. Follow this procedure through to the end of the video file, making sure the final row is blank but contains a start time as shown in **Figure 11.8**. This helps ensure that the exported caption file will work with all formats.

Figure 11.8. Make sure the last row does not contain a caption but does have a start time.

Once the file is complete, you can use the player controls to test your file and make sure your synchronization is accurate. Any changes you can make directly into the timecode of each starting point; just touch it and enter the new start time. Or you can rewind the video until it's in front of that caption, start play-back, and then press F9 when appropriate.

Now it's time to adjust the captions to the necessary justification (**Figure 11.9**). In this case, since I'm sitting on the left, I'll keep all my comments on the left, right-justify Ken's questions, and center-justify all other captions. If you didn't spell-check your captions in your word processor, you can access MAGpie's spell-check function by clicking Edit > Check Spelling in the main menu.

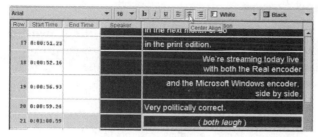

Figure 11.9.
Enter any changes directly in the timecode, then left, center, and right-justify the captions as required.

Because Ken and I were sitting still on our respective sides of the screen, I didn't insert any speaker names during the interview. Note that MAGpie reflects the Media Access Group's policy of isolating the speaker name on the first row of a caption, as shown in Figure 11.1. If you adopt a different policy, you can place the speaker name within the first row of the caption, so long as it's clearly distinguished from the spoken word.

Figure 11.10. MAGpie's preview screen.

Figure 11.10 contains the preview video from a 320x240 video produced in MAGpie. At 18 points, the text is reasonably readable and proportionate to the video. If you find your font size inappropriate, click File > Properties to return to the MAGpie Project Properties screen.

In terms of workflow, you can certainly enter captions directly into MAGpie if you choose, though I find it less efficient than creating a separate narration file in Word and then formatting that document for MAGpie. If you decide to enter the text directly into MAGpie, simply click the caption box to make the field active, and type the desired text. Use one carriage return to create another line within the caption, and a double carriage return to switch from caption to caption.

One final note. Though MAGpie is a free download, it proved very stable in my tests, performed on a Windows XP Professional computer (I did not test the Mac version). I encountered only one problem—I couldn't change justifications when working with 320x240 files, though this worked perfectly with 640x480 files.

Exporting the Captioned Stream

Exporting a file from MAGpie is simple; Click Export and choose the desired format (**Figure 11.11**). The only caveat is that MAGpie automatically overwrites any files in that directory without warning, so be careful to make sure there are no files in the path before exporting.

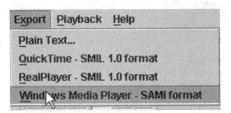

Figure 11.11.
Exporting caption files from MAGpie.

The Plain Text export feature is useful if you need a transcript of the event. Now that we have our exported captions properly formatted, it's time to mate them with our compressed video files to produce captioned video playback.

There are efforts underway to standardize how QuickTime, Real, and Windows Media files synchronize with text (see *www.w3.org/AudioVideo/timetext.html*), but until these standards are set and adopted by each company, you'll have to create a separate text file for each technology.

Closed Captioning and Windows Media Files

Using MAGpie's export function, I created interview.smi, a file compatible with Microsoft's Synchronized Accessible Media Interchange format, or SAMI (all SAMI files use the .SMI extension). This file contains the caption text and synchronization information just created in MAGpie. Now I'll create a text metafile with an .ASX extension to link this file with interview.wmv, the Windows Media file containing the streaming audio and video file.

To play the video concurrently with the closed caption file, viewers will load the ASX file into Media Player. Similarly, to post your video and captions to a Web site, you would upload all three files to your site and have your Web page link to the ASX file. More on that in a moment.

Here's what the ASX file contains in our simple example.

```
<ASX version="3.0">
<TITLE>Interview</TITLE>
<ENTRY>
<ABSTRACT>Discussion with Ken Santucci at NAB</ABSTRACT>
```

```
<TITLE>Interview</TITLE>
<AUTHOR>Jan Ozer</AUTHOR>
<COPYRIGHT>2004</COPYRIGHT>
<REF href="file://c:\interview.wmv?
SAMI=file://c:\interview.smi"
</ENTRY>
</ASX>
```

Figure 11.12 shows Windows Media Player displaying both the video file and the closed captions. On the right is the Content screen accessed by clicking File > Properties > Content tab, where you can see the Abstract, Title, and Author information mapping over from the ASX file.

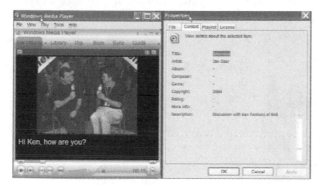

Figure 11.12.
Video and captions playing in Windows Media Player.

Windows Media Player won't play captions if you've selected a "skin" rather than being configured in Full mode. To return to Full mode, click View > Full Mode. In addition, Media Player won't play captions unless you enable the program to play captions. To do this, click Play > Captions and Subtitles > Captions. If your viewers can't see your captions, chances are it's one or both of these configuration issues causing the problem.

If you post the files to a Web site, you must upload the ASX, WMV, and SMI files to your server and update the ASX file to reflect the new locations (also called paths) of the content files. For an excellent white paper on ASX files, including paths to use for the various types of servers that support ASX files, check out *www.microsoft.com/netshow/howto/asx.htm.* To read up on the SAMI language, check out: *http://msdn.microsoft.com/library/default.asp?url=/library/en-us/dnwmt/html/wmp7_sami.asp.*

Finally, to learn how to embed Windows Media files directly into a Web site, see WebAIM's excellent description at *www.webaim.org/techniques/captions/windows/3?templatetype=3.*

Closed Captioning and Real Video Files

Where Microsoft uses ASX metafiles, RealVideo uses SMIL metafiles, which sound a lot happier (the word is actually pronounced "smile") but do pretty much the same thing: point RealPlayer to the video and caption file (called a RealText file with an RT extension). MAGpie makes life easy by producing both the SMIL file and the RT file during the same export procedure. To play the captioned stream, run RealPlayer and load the SMIL file MAGpie just created. You can see the results in **Figure 11.13**.

Since MAGpie creates the SMIL file automatically, I won't display it here. If you're curious, you should be able to open the file in any text editor. For more information on SMIL files, see the SMIL Web site at *www.w3.org/AudioVideo/*. WebAIM also explains how to link RealPlayer content at *www.webaim.org/techniques/captions/real/ 3?templatetype=3.*

Figure 11.13.
Since MAGpie creates all necessary files, you're ready to run RealPlayer and play the SMIL file.

Closed Captioning and QuickTime Files

MAGpie also produces two output files when exporting for QuickTime: a SMIL file that will play the video and captions together in QuickTime Player, and a text file containing the captions and synchronization information formatted in QuickTime format.

As with RealVideo, the SMIL file I produced for this interview loaded and played normally in QuickTime Player—no muss, no fuss. However, some producers like to add the captions directly into the MOV file containing the QuickTime video, resulting in one MOV file rather than three. Accomplishing this is a three-step process and you'll need QuickTime Professional to show you how ($29.99, direct from Apple).

Using QuickTime Pro, import the text file by clicking File > Import and selecting the text file. If the text imports properly, you should be able to play the text only file as shown in **Figure 11.14.**

Figure 11.14.
The captions file MAGpie created successfully imported into QuickTime Professional.

The next step is to copy and add the MOV file containing the text track into the MOV file containing the actual movie. In the text MOV you just created, click Edit > Select All to select the entire track, then copy it by clicking Edit > Copy.

Load the MOV file containing the audio and video into another QuickTime Player and click Edit > Add. QuickTime Pro adds the text track to the video file, but places it on top of the video (**Figure 11.15**).

The third step is to position the captions at the bottom. Click Movie > Get Movie Properties. Select the Text Track and Size, and then click the Adjust button. The text track will appear on top of the video with red scaling and rotation points. Grab any black part of the text track and drag it down until it's beneath the video track—it looks funky, but QuickTime will make room for it. Use your arrow keys to line up the text track precisely (**Figure 11.16**).

Figure 11.15.
Oops, captions are on top. Fix this in the Movie Properties screen.

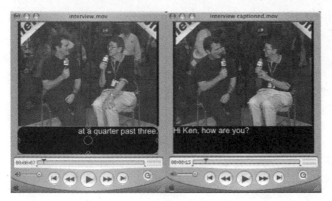

Figure 11.16.
Drag the captions down and align (on the left). The finished, captioned movie is on the right.

When finished, Click Done in the Movie Properties screen (where the Adjust button was) and save the file, making sure that it's self-contained. The finished captioned movie is shown on the right in Figure 11.16. Once again, you can find out more about embedding QuickTime files into a Web site at *www.webaim.org/ techniques/captions/quicktime/7.php*.

Converting Closed Captions to Subtitles

If you're producing streaming media with closed captions, chances are you're also producing DVDs using the same content. Obviously, once you've produced and synchronized the captions, you'd like to use the same files in your DVD productions. Once again, if you own a broadcast captioning program, start by asking your vendor if you can export DVD-compatible subtitles from their systems.

As I was working with MAGpie, this option wasn't open to me, so I started hunting around on the Web for a tool that could input closed captioned files, and output subtitle files compatible with the three authoring programs I primarily use, Adobe Encore 1.5, Apple's DVD Studio Pro 3, and Ulead's DVD Workshop 2.

My search wasn't exhaustive, but I soon found a program called Subtitle Workshop from URUSoft (*www.urusoft.net/products.php?cat=sw&lang=1*). The program is a free download; all the company asks is that satisfied users send donations via PayPal.

You can create subtitles in Subtitle Workshop, though it lacks features such as the ability to right- and left-justify text, and MAGpie's ability to synchronize captions to the video in real time. In terms of pure captioning usability, I preferred MAGpie. However, where MAGpie can only output in the three streaming video formats, Subtitle Workshop supports more than 50 DVD subtitle output formats and offers a wealth of import options.

I started by importing the SAMI file created by MAGpie, which formatted perfectly (**Figure 11.17**).

Figure 11.17.
Subtitle Workshop imported the SAMI file flawlessly.

Using the output templates available in Subtitle Workshop, I then exported caption files (File > Save As) for DVD Workshop and Adobe Encore. DVD Workshop imported the file without problem, though I had to perform minor text cleanup, primarily in two-line captions, which DVD Workshop attempted to display in one line (you'll notice it truncated "been digitized" to "beedigitized" in **Figure 11.18**). In addition, all captions were center-justified and placed in the middle of the screen.

When I attempted to import the captions into Adobe Encore, I received the error message shown in **Figure 11.19**. Apparently, Encore can only import Unicode files.

I loaded the file into Windows Notepad to see if I could spot any obvious errors, then checked Notepad's export options to see if either option recommended by the Encore error message was available. If you click File > Save As, then the Encoding drop-down list box, you'll see that UTF-8 is listed. I saved the file into UTF-8 format, and Encore loaded it without problem (**Figure 11.20**) and all captions displayed correctly, though they were all left-justified and placed on the left of the screen.

Interestingly, Encore's workflow for caption creation is comparatively weak, so budget-minded producers adding subtitles to their DVDs should consider using the MAGpie-to-Subtitle Workshop workflow.

Figure 11.18.
The subtitles imported into DVD Workshop without difficulty but required some minor text cleanup.

Figure 11.19.
Looks like Encore needs a Unicode file.

Figure 11.20.
Mission accomplished: captions appear in Adobe Encore.

Importing into DVD Studio Pro required a bit more trial and error, but was ultimately successful. We first tried the DVD Studio Pro output preset, which wouldn't import. This wasn't surprising given that Apple had changed the subtitle architecture in Version 3. Fortunately, the Apple manual outlines several other formats that should import, including the Spruce Technologies STL format (DVD Studio Pro is partly based on a defunct program called Spruce DVD Maestro).

We tried that format and DVD Studio Pro happily accepted it, with a couple of minor problems—primarily replacing a <P> with a carriage return to produce a two-line caption. As with DVD Workshop, all captions were center-justified and placed in the bottom center of the screen.

While not totally problem-free, Subtitle Workshop certainly proved much more efficient than starting from scratch, and you have to like the price! Subtitle Workshop is not the only fish in the caption-converting sea, however. I also found a product called Lemony (*www.jorgemorones.com/lemony/index.htm*) that can import MAGpie files and output captions for DVD authoring in a variety of formats, and (it costs €135 from Europe).

In the Workbook

The workbook for this chapter includes program-specific instructions for inserting and creating closed captions in supported DVD authoring programs. Go to *www.doceo.com/dv101.html* for a list of currently supported authoring programs.

Index

X

XLR connector, 20
XLRM connector, 25
XLR-to-3.5mm connector
   Beachtek DXA-8, 26
   line-matching transformer, 25
   Shure A96F transformer, 26

Z

zebra pattern, defined, 54
zooming, effect on streaming
quality, 8